Bugle Call

STEWARDSHIP IS SERIOUS BUSINESS

Caring for our Communities
Requires Deep Thought
and Purposeful Action

Deborah Jane Nankivell

ISBN: 1501010905
ISBN 13: 9781501010903

DEDICATION

This book is dedicated to the five presidents
of the Fresno Business Council.
My teachers, colleagues, coaches and dear friends.
But for you—I would have remained a disembodied voice.

Richard Johanson
Ken Newby
Dr. Alan Pierrot
Dr. John Welty
Scott Rhodes

Also to
Kurt Madden
Douglas E. Noll
Michael Wilhelm
Morgan Family Foundation
California Stewardship Network

And
Noelle Tuley Rickel
Scout

CONTENTS

PREFACE

Richard A. Johanson

As you eagerly turn the pages of this fascinating chronicle, it is my hope that you will, as I did, discover a similarity between civic transformation and the creation of a concert orchestra.

This book describes the emergence of those residing within and near Fresno, California, from listening to a group of well-intentioned but disconnected, often-discordant soloists into enjoying a vibrant regional symphonic assembly of inspired, highly skilled community stewards.

Slightly over twenty years ago, Deborah Nankivell arrived in Fresno from Minnesota. She quickly learned that this region was better known for its social, educational and public administration shortcomings than for its considerable strengths.

She also found, however, a small group of individuals committed to changing that. It was in that context that in 1993 she became the CEO of the newly formed Fresno Business Council, a position that she still holds.

Many council members were excellent "soloists" who had never worked together. As they began to realize that by performing as an ensemble they would attract a wider audience, they gathered others with similar talents to join with them.

Today the Fresno Business Council and its partners are passionate performers of "concerts" attracting attention as an approach to community transformation through unselfish interaction.

Every successful orchestra must be inspired and conducted by an individual possessing the skill, passion and commitment to mold its components into an effective entity.

I am extremely pleased and honored to present to you my dear friend Maestro Deborah J. Nankivell.

Richard A. Johanson, chair emeritus of the Fresno Business Council, is a Marine combat veteran of World War II. His books *A Passion for Stewardship: The Legacy of a Generation* and *Just a Thought: Reflections on Civic Transformation* offer perspectives on the responsibilities of citizens and the story of Fresno.

FORWARD

In the late 1990s, my colleague Curtis Johnson and I received a fascinating invitation from John W. Gardner, fabled former Cabinet Secretary, foundation president, founder of Common Cause and other renowned civic institutions, Presidential Medal of Freedom awardee. Would we, Gardner asked, write a report showing how a sampling of American cities are making their civic process work?

"The key," he wrote introducing the booklet we produced, "is to get people talking and working together across the boundary lines that traditionally divide and diminish a community – people from government, corps, social agencies, ethnic groups, unions, neighborhoods." Because, he wrote, "building healthy communities is less about structure and more about building relationships. Relationship building is the key to breaking political gridlock and being able to take action in the public interest."

Inspired by Gardner – and the living experiences we found in cities ranging from Chattanooga to Kansas City to Denver to San Diego – we decided to title our booklet *Boundary Crossing*, with a subhead: *Community Leadership in a Global Age*.

As the reader will discover in these pages, Deborah Nankivell is a boundary crosser *par excellence*. She has had terrific allies including the business "lions" she's worked so closely with. But her perseverance, her vision, in creating alliances across professional, educational, city and neighborhood boundaries sings from these pages.

It's not surprising that Nankivell selects a group of choice John Gardner quotes to illustrate her points. What is astounding is how, without taking explicit credit, she has personally been key to one important civic connection after another. How she's helped business work in a challenged city and region with rare sensitivity and effectiveness. And now, for us, outlines the foundation – intellectual, patriotic and passionate – of what she senses and defines as the *sacred space* of American community.

Neal R. Peirce
Journalist
Chairman, the Citistates Group
Founder and editor-in-chief of Citiscope.

INTRODUCTION

Many of us remember moments when our childhood beliefs were crushed by reality. We learned that life isn't fair and bad things happen to everyone. We realized there were times when our parents did not know the answers nor did anyone else. We had to find out for ourselves. For me, one of the most jarring awakenings was when I realized that what I believed about America wasn't true.

I wrote this book for everyone who lives with nagging angst about his or her community and our country. For those who want to do something about it but don't know how. It's for those who care deeply about our children, our planet and our survival.

You're not alone and you can't fix what's wrong by yourself. Together we can create what we truly want. Together we can experience the American Dream of liberty and justice for all.

This is a book about personal and community transformation through freedom fighting and selfless stewardship. It explains what it means to be an American citizen in heart, mind and deed, undocumented or not, on American soil or not. We are about liberating the human spirit from bondage and acceding to freedom's demands for eternal vigilance.

This book seeks to:

- Capture the story of a team of people who have tenaciously sought to improve economic, social and environmental conditions of the San Joaquin Valley.
- Be a primer for community transformation based upon what we have learned.
- Be a compass and source of inspiration in facing a path likely to pass through unexpected hazards and test everyone's endurance.
- Offer hope to the discouraged and a path of action for those who want to help.

I wrote this book because I live every day grateful that I live in a country inspired by ideals of what is possible for humanity and for the amazing people who have stepped up and sacrificed so much to make it so.

Sometimes all you have is the courage to hope. In Fresno, we have learned that is enough.

Those who engage in the work create a new space by simply stepping into the civic sector, which is sacred space in a democracy. Here labels, history, socioeconomics, gender and race are irrelevant. This space is where We The People come together as equals to govern ourselves; where leaders emerge, only because others choose to follow them.

In Fresno, we call this space the Fourth Sphere.

While not everyone has the capacity to think or lead from this space, everyone has a citizen's responsibility to support it as the price of freedom.

Growing up in a small Wisconsin city and very patriotic home, I sang the *Star-Spangled Banner* with great enthusiasm and took to heart the belief I lived in "the home of brave." As the shadow side of our history seeped into my awareness, I felt betrayed.

Then, one day it occurred to me America was truly a dream. It existed in the mind, the heart and the soul of those who believed we could govern ourselves, be free to create our own lives and work together to produce the beloved community.

It would be up to every generation to build upon past progress and lessons learned to move closer to a great civilization offering liberty and justice for all. While many don't believe it possible, given weaknesses in human nature, we do. Freedom fighting demands courage and passion whether taking a hill, challenging corruption or facing our own deceit.

The tide is turning, but those who are not engaged in transformation work are unlikely to know about it. I use the word transformation to mean a change in form, appearance, nature or character based upon a commitment to defined shared values and an inspiring vision. The new DNA will yield a new reality when fully manifested.

I regularly think about symbols of our country in Washington, D.C. – monuments to some of our greatest victories, tributes to those willing to die to achieve them and reminders of some of our gravest missteps.

I am grateful also for so many in my adopted community, Fresno, who welcomed me and share my passion for freedom in community. We believe that united we can create what truly matters to all of us – the experience of belonging, love and purpose, which are the ingredients of a high quality of life. Peace and prosperity are the natural byproducts.

Like all stories, this is told through the eyes of the writer as filtered by life experiences and beliefs. I moved to Fresno in 1993 after a life already rich with diverse experiences and an unwavering belief in what our higher selves could create together. I had also experienced the shadow side of people disconnected and with no sense of responsibility to others. While I have been influenced and enriched by those I have met or know through their writings, what I say is my interpretation of events and ideas.

In the story, I play a number of roles, primarily as catalyst. I had fully embraced the culture of Minnesota before coming to Fresno. I believed in taking responsibility as an individual and the importance of community. Having been in recovery from trauma since I was twenty-five, I also have a deep commitment to living with integrity and am inspired by Gandhi's challenge to be the change we wanted to see in the world. I have finely tuned Midwestern, middle-class values and the optimism and work ethic that accompany them.

The contrasts between the Twin Cities and Fresno were stark in nearly every way in 1993. Both have amazing assets and challenges yet unmet. No community can rest on past success or be limited by past failures. Change requires believing in possibility and demanding eternal vigilance.

California was not what I expected, where the San Joaquin Valley contains some of the most concentrated poverty in the United States. Agriculture-based industries that pay low wages and employ substantial numbers of immigrants predominate and there are relatively few high-wage opportunities. This results in thousands of households living below the poverty line.

Poverty can be tied to the unintended consequence of federal, state and local policies, combined with decades of denial, neglect and exploitation. Together they have created a dismaying level of despair, social problems and environmental degradation within what I had believed was the Golden State.

California led the way in allowing such unacceptable circumstances to fester, albeit largely hidden from view for decades. Allowing poverty to become chronic demonstrates the extensive gap between our values and our behavior, inflaming those who rightfully call out our hypocrisy.

Men of integrity, by their very existence, rekindle the belief that as a people
we can live above the level of moral squalor. We need that belief; a
cynical community is a corrupt community. John W. Gardner

This story is about a team of people and a growing network of individuals who decided to do something about it. It took years to unbundle and better understand the complexity of our challenges and to develop an alternative approach that looks promising.

Pioneering efforts are by their nature disruptive, often misunderstood and inherently risky. It has been difficult to secure resources to attract the level of talent we need. However, this financial struggle has resulted in a scrappy, duct-tape approach that has strengthened us, built trust and solidified our foundation. Now we are attracting more people and resources to the work.

I have come to appreciate that while we may be inspired by another community's story – and I hope you will be – every community has to find its own path, choosing what it needs from another's experience.

"Most of the important things in the world have been accomplished by people who have kept on trying when there
seemed to be no hope at all." Dale Carnegie

Holding onto a vision when there is little evidence it will ever happen requires a depth of commitment few seem capable of maintaining. I count on poetry to remind and renew me, as Scots poet Sir Walter Scott does, so I never lose sight that we all stand on the shoulders of others.

The Lay of the Last Minstrel—Sir Walter Scott

Breathes there the man with soul so dead
Who never to himself hath said,

This is my own, my native land!
Whose heart hath ne'er within him burned,
As home his footsteps he hath turned
From wandering on a foreign strand!
If such there breathe, go, mark him well;
For him no minstrel raptures swell;
High though his titles, proud his name,
Boundless his wealth as wish can claim
Despite those titles, power, and pelf,
The wretch, concentred all in self,
Living, shall forfeit fair renown,
And, doubly dying, shall go down
To the vile dust from whence he sprung,
Unwept, unhonored, and unsung.

Another poem has haunted me since I memorized it in ninth grade, *O Captain! My Captain!*, the most popular poem of Walt Whitman and written through his pain following the death of Abraham Lincoln.

O Captain! My Captain!—Walt Whitman

O Captain! my Captain! our fearful trip is done,
The ship has weathered every rack, the prize we sought is won,
The port is near, the bells I hear, the people all exulting,
While follow eyes the steady keel, the vessel grim and daring;
But O heart! heart! heart!
O the bleeding drops of red,
Where on the deck my Captain lies,
Fallen cold and dead.

O Captain! my Captain! rise up and hear the bells;
Rise up–for you the flag is flung–for you the bugle trills,
For you bouquets and ribboned wreaths–for you the shores a-crowding,
For you they call, the swaying mass, their eager faces turning;

Here Captain! dear father! This arm beneath your head!
It is some dream that on the deck
You've fallen cold and dead.

My captain does not answer; his lips are pale and still,
My father does not feel my arm; he has no pulse nor will,
The ship is anchored safe and sound, its voyage closed and done,
From fearful trip the victor ship comes in with object won;
Exult, O shores, and ring O bells!
But I, with mournful tread,
Walk the deck my Captain lies,
Fallen cold and dead.

These inspiring words about triumph over despair remind us that standing on principles of liberty and equality may lead to death, and also that those who sacrifice anonymously so that others can live in freedom reach a higher platform. I can neither read nor recite either poem without tears in my eyes and a catch in my throat.

PART ONE—FRESNO: SMALL ENOUGH TO DO IT; BIG ENOUGH TO MATTER

Chapter 1

SETTING THE TABLE

To achieve transformation, I've learned we need lots of different people on the team:

- Some learn best through stories. They're not people of action but play the essential role of historians and culture keepers.
- Others just want the tools and a map so they can get to work, plow through a to-do list and deliver results that are easy to measure.
- People bent on action often have little patience for visionaries and strategic thinkers who want to reflect deeply about purpose, long-term implications and the best way to approach something.
- Some need a clearly marked path to venture off a beaten trail – happy to execute as long as the guidelines are clear.
- Entrepreneurial individuals learn to fail fast and adapt quickly to dead ends or changing conditions.

The challenge to assembling a highly functional team is learning to value and embed the gifts of all in the thinking and doing, which takes time and patience, particularly when most of the players are volunteers. What we ask of everyone lies beyond their job descriptions or pay grades. We need them to assume the responsibilities of citizens, offering their highest-level skills, resources and positional influence to serve the whole community.

In Fresno, years of working together have enabled us to tap a deep reservoir of gifts and talents to create a leadership circle. We now understand that while leadership is important to achieve measurable results, stewardship is the key to transformation.

Over time, stewards take responsibility for the whole whether they hold a position of leadership or not. Their inner compass is intact. They tend to the seeds – values, mindsets and culture – while simultaneously advancing tactics that lead to the fruit, both measurable and intangible.

Becoming a community steward involves working alongside others, taking the time to understand how the community works and sharing one's highest-level skills to achieve a common agenda. Most have been deeply changed by the experience.

Passing the torch is a common and important symbol of embracing change and releasing power to the next generation, which is expected to step up and perform its role. In some parts of the U.S., a sense of anonymity and fragmentation grew and the stewardship pipeline seemed to evaporate as leaders seemed more interested in personal ambitions then the fate of their nation or community.

Interdependence ebbed as a sense of isolation, mean-spirited competition and limitations flowed. A deepening angst eroded shared sense of purpose, described by Robert Putnam in *Bowling Alone: The Collapse and Revival of American Community.*

In Fresno, we have been in the midst of a community revival for over a decade, becoming intentional about passing the torch, while gaining an understanding of key issues and experimenting with various ways to address them. We progressed from a handful of Fresno leaders hoping for improvement, to a broad, tenacious effort to improve the economic, social and environmental conditions of the San Joaquin

Valley. What we did right and wrong, what we have yet to accomplish form a primer for community transformation.

There are a number of words and concepts we have defined for ourselves, while learning also that a shared glossary is important to building trust and communicating effectively. While we are one community – one family as it were – we are rich in difference. We are multicultural, speak many languages and have unique stories. Our shared glossary has helped build bridges necessary to work together across sectors, disciplines and tribes. We are creating a new culture and are proving that words shared again and again can change the thinking and behavior of individuals and eventually give birth to a new norm.

Earlier in America, all members of the community played a role in building barns, which were essential to the prosperity of families and to the community as a whole. Interdependence was a lived reality in which most participants were volunteers, and a handful of people with special skills were paid. This is the approach we've followed in Fresno.

Overall coordination and leadership functions are essential. These leaders along with experts help turn our good intentions, unrealized plans and money spent on tactics with limited impact into transformational change that alters underlying conditions and develops those who have become mired in them.

America's civic space seemed to be abandoned after World War II. Baby-boomers never quite stepped up to lead with the deep sense of unity, purpose and dignity that marked the World War II generation. Possibly, the Vietnam War, Watergate scandal, the Kennedy assassinations and the Rev. Martin Luther King Jr.'s murder conspired in our descent into self-absorption, denial and consumption.

Of course, not everyone shirked their responsibilities to family and community, but enough boomers did so I am often defensive, sad and resolute all at once when asked what happened to my generation. Yes, we challenged hypocrisy and many served in a terrible war, but some of us lived in what we now understand as dysfunctional families, rife with secrets and stifled by roles and scripts that didn't allow their full bloom as individuals. As we have reached later mid-life, an awakening to purpose is building. Many who have been successful in the market place are searching for ways to use their skills and resources to serve their communities. Encouragingly, the generations coming behind are engaging as well, addressing issues such as health care, poverty, job creation and education that have seemed insolvable for so long.

We offer Fresno's story as one example, some of which may be replicable in other communities. More likely residents within each community will discover their own formula for transformation. However, there are fundamentals that we must remember to keep the American story alive. Values, vision and spirit remain when the people, structures and systems fade away. Positive ideas not dwelling on negative reality ignite the passion needed to take action. Making the American Dream come true is an interdependent commitment that requires individual and collective determination.

To help learn as much as possible about transformational community building, I have tapped a wealth of knowledge and wisdom, but three in particular have inspired my journey: John W. Gardner, Ayn Rand and Anne Frank. I've struggled to resolve the paradoxes between rights and responsibilities of community and the individual. My willingness to see the best in others protected my belief in a better world. Rand's fierceness, her love of America and the scars from her experience of Communism branded my mind with a commitment to capitalism. Making my way around the circle of life, I realized that Gardner, Rand and Frank were basically speaking to the same issues but looking at them through the lenses of their lives.

This book – and life itself – is about the liberation of the human spirit.

America's greatness has been the greatness of a free people who shared certain moral commitments. Freedom without moral commitment is aimless and promptly self-destructive. John W. Gardner

Chapter 2

OLD WAYS NO LONGER WORK—

NOW WHAT?

Like many business civic groups, the Fresno Business Council was formed to fill a perceived leadership vacuum in a community where juvenile crime was out of control and social and economic indicators were in a downward spiral. In times of crisis, senior business leaders often step into the civic sector to grapple with serious issues. I think of this as the lion spirit, the totem that when awakened cannot be ignored.

The "lions" of the Fresno Business Council have guided the organization since its founding, ensuring that it held to its higher purpose. While this view was not uniformly shared by members, the lions worked hard to keep our focus on the community and to prevent distractions from self-serving or single interests of members, politicians or funders. Thanks to their leadership, the organization remains dynamic, entrepreneurial and committed to the principles of stewardship.

Some business-driven civic groups focus primarily on business-environment issues. While essential to a vibrant economy, that approach limits focus and may miss opportunities. Who will ensure that government, schools and neighborhoods are high functioning if those with the most developed skills and the greatest influence avoid the public and political realms? A demand of citizenship is that all contribute at their highest level of impact.

> *"Every community has enough leaders to run a small nation, but they're not leading. They are hiding out, living comfortable lives giving little or no attention to the current and future problems of their community. Who gave them permission to stand aside?"*
> John W. Gardner

The Fresno Business Council's inaugural retreat in 1993 was led by a respected leader of the reinventing government movement. Mostly high-powered CEOs, council members had little patience with his process orientation and contextual focus. They wanted action. So the group sent him packing. At a reinventing government conference in Minneapolis he ran into a Fresno based consultant and confided his perplexity at the behavior of the Fresno leaders. The Fresno consultant was not at all surprised. Change agents, creative thinkers and intellectuals had bounced off Fresno's psychic hard pan (the San Joaquin Valley's concrete like soil layer) for years. I can attest that new leaders are often embraced at first, then forced to run a gauntlet of doubt before they can settle in and join with others committed to transformation. Those lacking the fortitude for this passage often leave and tell Fresno tales to whomever will listen.

Having taken over their own retreat, the "mutineers" set their own priorities, chose issue leaders and left to take charge of their community confident in their power to tell others what to do and willing to spend money to carry out their plans. They hired another consultant to develop a financing strategy, but with an economy that competes largely on low cost and commodities, paying for value was not the dominant culture and the fund-raising effort failed. The group recalibrated to cobble together the necessary resources on their own.

With more work, the council president's office staff could no longer handle the load. The executive committee decided to hire a coordinator. I was working in the founder's office as a lobbyist and was asked to take the position on a part-time basis. It was a good fit as I did not want to put my 4 year old daughter into fulltime day care and helping to organize a nonprofit fit my skills. However, years as the executive director of Common Cause Minnesota had made me cautious about the intentions of the private sector in community change.

I was sobered by Fresno's challenges, which appeared to have no civic sector and no platform where the community could come together to solve problems and cast visions. The positional leaders didn't trust one another and most improvement efforts were fragmented. Over time, attempts to address a wide range of issues and crises had led to a crazy quilt of organizations and projects lacking strategic or transformational purpose.

Where there is no vision, the people will perish.
Proverbs 29:18

Many leaders simply drew linear conclusions without deeply understanding the problems, dismissing reflection and study as "not doing anything." They are not stewards. They may get things done, but too often they're the wrong things done the wrong way inviting a strong and often successful adverse reaction. The work of community is deep. The work of a broken community is deeper still.

Political extremism involves two prime ingredients: an excessively simple diagnosis of the world's ills, and a conviction that there are identifiable villains back of it all.
John. W. Gardner

The early years of the Fresno Business Council were mostly about gaining a better understanding of issues, people and the business of the community and also building relationships, often called social capital. There were discrete projects – helping create the Central Valley

Business Incubator and Center for Advanced Research and Technology – but most efforts followed a traditional pattern of standing committees, guest speakers and small projects.

Like many communities, board and committee service for most business people was about social and professional networking. Nonprofits addressed symptoms of poverty, ill health or lack of education or promoted single issues like the environment, cultural arts or sports. There was no central hub to align the disparate parts into a shared strategy to reach the heart of the matter and transform the status quo.

While my academic and professional careers only marginally touched upon economics, I have become fascinated by various perspectives and their impact on a community. An economy built upon principles of Monopoly® leads to winners and losers. Liberty and justice for all requires a game based upon the principles of Abundant Community, a term used by consultants John McKnight and Peter Block, where those with greatest abilities and work ethic still achieve the success they deserve. Everyone's gifts are valued, and those who cannot earn a living – as opposed to those who will not – are supported through a tightly woven safety net. Critical to a healthy social contract is that our actions do not cause harm to others physically, emotionally or financially. This applies to individuals, organizations and businesses alike.

Interdependence runs counter to Monopoly because:
- More, cheaper and faster are not better when products cause harm, costs are externalized to the environment and communities and activists defend them with lawsuits and regulations.
- A hypercompetitive, materialistic culture is unhealthy for most people and can bring out the worst in those equipped to succeed in it.
- Individuals and groups in need that fall through the cracks may never develop and contribute their gifts, becoming tax burdens as welfare recipients or through criminal activity.

- Some simply retire on the job – public or private – never reaching full potential or making much of a contribution, perhaps because they're uncomfortable with the values of the system they're in and unsure what to do about it.

We all have bills to pay and families to support, but I wonder if some simply forgot or never learned the price others paid for freedom. A life of quiet desperation serves no one.

Chapter 3

PLAN B. A BETTER WAY—COLLABORATION

The Fresno Business Council's first major initiative aimed to improve land use decisions, which had previously conspired to concentrate the prosperous and the poor and to create unaffordable infrastructure and maintenance costs for the city. We teamed with the American Farmland Trust, Farm Bureau, Chamber of Commerce and Building Industry Association to craft *A Landscape of Choice—Strategies For Improving Patterns of Community Growth* released in 1998.

Our collaboration was national news, marking a coming together of organizations led by community-minded people who recognized that past patterns were unsustainable and unjust. While we lacked the technical expertise, resources and platform to execute many of the concepts, we had planted seeds for support of future regional Smart Growth land-use planning efforts including the *San Joaquin Valley Blueprint* and *Smart Valley Places*.

In 2012, the Fresno City Council voted to incorporate Smart Growth principles in the General Plan update. This significant milestone was accomplished because equity advocates spent hours coaching residents in low-income areas about Smart Growth and the role they could play in improving their neighborhoods.

Residents showed up en masse at the hearings. People with limited English and no prior engagement bravely took the podium to support a better future for their community, joined by business, agriculture, equity advocates and the general community. Now, the challenge is commitment to sustaining the collaboration.

One important learning from the *Landscape of Choice* effort was the importance of stewards in developing public policies and leading institutions. Short of that, policies are much more likely to be distorted to achieve narrow, short-term goals of single and self-interested individuals, which can cause profound harm to a community. Stewardship embraces a broader approach that promotes the strategic alignment necessary to address complex, interdependent issues so they do not become chronic and eventually accepted as inevitable.

In general, the private sector develops business models to achieve the greatest profit possible, believing that profit leads to wealth creation, salary and benefit increases, research, and taxes to support government essentials and corporate philanthropy.

While profit's a good thing, policies can become harmful if distorted through single-focus influence and allowing companies to externalize their costs to other businesses, employees, citizens or the environment. The larger these interests become, the more likely they will concentrate attention at the legislative and Congressional levels, electing people who think first of serving those who paid for their campaigns rather than the best interests of the community they were elected to serve.

Not just the private sector, but single interests of all kinds – personal, financial, social or environmental – often seek to advance their own short-term objectives, even if unwittingly, rather than thinking as citizens first. Only those who start from a commitment to the whole are prepared for the hard work of balancing interests in collaboration that leads to sustainable results.

While there were successes, we realized that we could never *do* enough to overcome a *being* problem. In other words, the dominant culture – how the majority thought and acted – stood in the way of solutions. Transformational change by addressing the seed causes at the level of thought and belief would be required to substantially improve the community.

Many of the founders still operated from the existing paradigm but were open to the possibility that something new and less-linear must be embraced. Sometimes a direct causal relationship is an accurate perception inviting clear and easily measurable solutions. However, human beings are complex, multidimensional and messy beings who often don't understand why we do what we do, much less what motivates others.

The Watchman's Rattle—Thinking Our Way Out of Extinction underscores why our current level of thinking is not equipped to meet our challenges. As author Rebecca Costa points out, major civilizations have reached this point and then disappeared as they resorted to voodoo type solutions to manage their mounting fear and confusion. She suggests that answers would most likely come from the two percent of the population that have an innate ability to think outside of time and space. Depending upon ones perspective, these people are often called visionaries, shamans, or crazy.

I believe Western culture, long separated from its heart and soul, has reached such a juncture because of materialism, the mothership of all addictions. It's futile to look outside of oneself to feel better or solve problems that only deep understanding and responsive action can resolve. Leading and allowing personal or collective change requires courage, humility and a willingness to map a course with no guarantees of success. Those who have benefitted most from the status quo, also require a spirit of generosity and gratitude.

A handful of the founders opened the door to new approaches by allowing others to use their social and professional relationships. The lion spirit in Fresno was most powerfully embodied in three men I dubbed The Lions – Robert Duncan, James Hallowell and Richard Johanson. While as an organization we focus on principles and values rather than personalities and positions, when principles become embodied in people they become visible and provide role models.

I believe the lion spirit exists in every community and in response to crisis will awaken. Our challenge is to sustain their spirit by following their example of selfless, thoughtful, collaborative discernment and informed action.

The Fresno Business Council might be as unique among the nation's civic business organizations as the circumstances that called it forth. It emerged in an isolated large city in one of the poorest and most-neglected regions of the country where some resources, including those possible through Fortune 500-level CEOs and their companies, are unavailable. The small businesses and regional offices that are the backbone of the economy are resourceful. The Fresno Business Council adopted a duct tape, do-it-ourselves approach, creating strengths and relationships that probably would not have occurred had there been an easier way. My image is Apollo 13. When the alarm sounded and those on earth thought at first the astronauts didn't have the tools they needed to return home, "Well, we're all gonna die!" roused everyone from their stupor of limited thinking and a safe, if inelegant safe return resulted.

It was choosing to not be victims and held hostage to our problems, looking instead for readiness, talent and resources to work together and solve them, that created our path.

Chapter 4

SPEAKING TRUTH TO POWER—

GO FOR BROKE

The Fresno Business Council was created to be nonpartisan and apolitical. However, these commitments were tested early when the community elected a mayor backed by business interests. He believed in a very limited role for government, wanted to cut services to the bone, rejected the possibility of public-private partnerships and demonstrated great difficulty working with anyone who disagreed with him.

After the FBC's plea to reconsider his approach, I joined a diverse group of people in an effort to recall him. Because the FBC board had determined that individuals could do what they wanted but the organization would not take a stand, I offered my resignation. The board rejected my offer on the condition that I not be public about my decision.

The recall effort put a tremendous strain on the organization. Some board members feared the controversy would fracture the group, leading to its demise. In the end, only one member quit. The council Lions courageously went public with their support of a better future for the community, standing on principle while recognizing there could be social, financial or other consequences.

The recall failed, but it did signal the business community's willingness to take on difficult tasks. Business, union and community leaders had challenged the existing conflict of interest, self-interest and single interests culture and some stepped up to serve the community as stewards, setting the stage for sustained transformation and adaptation. Today, there are many more steward leaders at varying stages of development. We have become intentional about discovering stewards amid our diverse leaders including younger generations to feed a stewardship pipeline essential to community success.

Chapter 5

UPPING OUR GAME, GOING
AFTER THE IMPOSSIBLE

A major shift for the Fresno Business Council occurred in 1999 when the Great Valley Center released *Economic Future of the San Joaquin Valley*, a report written by Collaborative Economics. It challenged the community to choose its future: Stick with an economy based upon a single industry competing largely on low cost and continue deteriorating social and economic conditions or make a fundamental shift toward diversification and innovation.

We recruited a New Economy Task Force that reflected members' intellect, diverse experiences, integrity and wit. We met every week for four months sorting through our options to answer one question: What initiatives would have such powerful rippling impact that they would transform the community by increasing per capita earned income to at least the state average?

We called these initiatives the "dominoes" and they focused on ubiquitous broadband, increasing knowledge workers, smart growth and transportation, shifting to an innovation culture and improving human development systems. Launching a water technology industry cluster was part of the package of activities. As testament to the depth of personal commitment to this work, a number of the taskforce members continue to play active roles.

As Fresno charted a new course for its future, Nick Bollman of the James Irvine Foundation envisioned a new course for California. He and others came up with the concept of the three Es – economy, environment and equity. Then Bollman persuaded the Irvine Foundation to invest seed capital in forward-thinking experiments in a dozen regions, each based upon locally devised customized ideas. In addition to their local work, the leaders of the regional efforts were brought together annually to share their experiences and best practices.

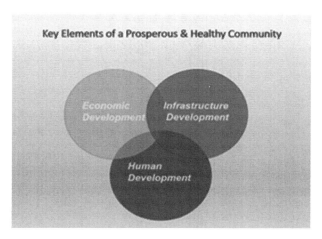

The region had a history of weak organizations that competed with one another for limited resources and were driven by a scarcity mind-set. Although relatively new, the Fresno Business Council was identified by the Irvine Foundation as capable to develop the three Es in the San Joaquin Valley. The graphic is an illustration of Fresno's version of the three Es.

The FBC and California State University, Fresno teamed up to create something new, a virtual organization supported as a joint venture – the Fresno Area Collaborative Regional Initiative (CRI). Central to this collaboration was Fresno State President John D. Welty, a founding member of the FBC, whose passion was to engage the university's assets in service to community needs.

With no agenda save community transformation, the council has been able to maintain a laser focus on it. And while the FBC doesn't often get credit, many things would not have happened without its existence. Ribbon cutting and stone cutting are vastly different levels of engagement in terms of time and understanding.

> *"When nothing seems to help, I go and look at a*
> *stonecutter hammering away at his*
> *rock perhaps a hundred times without as much as a crack showing in it.*
> *Yet at the hundred and first blow it will split in*
> *two, and I know it was not that blow*
> *that did it, but all that had gone before."* – Jacob August Riis

A package of great ideas, financial resources and high-level talent may result in amazing achievements, but it does not guarantee transformational change, which requires a leader with a certain mindset and unique set of skills for success. Ashley Swearengin stepped up as chief operating officer of the Collaborative Regional Initiative and Welty offered to house and fund her at Fresno State's Central Valley Futures Institute. Swearengin was able to tap university resources and recruit community organizations and individuals to implement the CRI's five major initiatives, embracing 26 projects. The Futures Institute morphed into the Office of Community and Economic Development as the agenda expanded.

With just a half-page memorandum of understanding, Swearengin and I used the CRI to serve the entire community. While we were clearly collaborating, it went deeper. Instead of working together because it is required, practical or the preferred strategy, Swearengin and I held similar beliefs. The level of commitment we experienced comes from the heart, resistant to pressure that serves a particular organization or issue at the expense of the whole. Some will step back from integrity when there could be a personal cost – position, relationship or money – but when you begin at the level of communion, compromising principles or self-interested decisions are not optional.

21

Once five dominos were selected, initiative leaders recruited and the task forces populated, the core leadership team scheduled a launch retreat in the Sierra east of Fresno for in September of 2001. Changing the dominant culture was deemed critical to success, so we set out to adopt a new contract for behavior connected to inspiring qualities Swearengin and I saw in FBC members. The CRI established core community values: stewardship, boundary crossing and collaboration, commitment to outcomes, fact-based decision-making, truth-telling, art-of-the-possible thinking, power parity and dedication to resolving conflict. We later added asset-based approach and disclosing conflicts of interest.

The chronological proximity of our retreat to the horror of the 9/11 terrorist attacks had profound impact on the retreat's participants and the outcomes. We were deeply aware of our shared humanity and intertwined fates as we thought about what our future might hold. Community values – already invoking higher and deeper thinking – became deeply embedded in the participants. Einstein wisely taught us, "You cannot solve a problem on the level of thinking that created it," but he did not explain how to get there. Values offer a ladder to the changes we've enjoyed continuously in the thinking and the behavior of many of those active in our community. Over time, if we continue to persevere, our hope is that the dominant culture will too.

Nick Bollman from the Irvine Foundation and Doug Henton, founder of Collaborative Economics, attended the retreat to offer their insights into the CRI movement, providing the outside prophets and validation so often needed for change efforts. Intellectual capital provided by colleagues outside of the region has proven to be invaluable.

While the genesis of transformational change was built upon the social capital of founders of the FBC, particularly our Lions, we relied on knowledge from outside the area to figure out what to do. "Brain drain" in the region was not just about those with talent leaving or not being attracted to the area, it also meant that those with advanced intellectual skills were unwelcome in the civic sector because their new ideas threatened the status quo. Thanks to the well-tilled soil of social capital generated by the Lions, this time the intellectual capital took root.

As an off-radar effort, the CRI attracted a network of people interested in community betterment. Teams driving the five initiatives developed projects to achieve the overriding goal of each domino. Because interdependence was an underlying theme, shared meetings and communication links were central to identifying leveraging opportunities.

The Innovation and Knowledge Worker and Human Investment teams aimed at changing the mindset of the community and improving skills across a spectrum of disciplines. Innovation created InForum to bring cutting-edge thinkers to the community to inspire new levels of thought. Another key project, *The New Valley Times*, was a newspaper from the future (2015) published in the Fresno Bee, detailing all the amazing things that had happened as a result of the actions begun in 2000. It caused quite a stir with a dateline in the future.

The land-use team built upon the earlier collaborative document *A Landscape of Choice,* which brought the concept of Smart Growth to the Fresno area. Seeds from this effort continue to bear fruit. The regional and local Blueprint projects, both comprehensive-planning efforts, continue to gain traction. As one of the three E's, environment includes the built and natural environment necessary to build and sustain a strong economy and high quality of place.

The Human Investment team laid a foundation for later, more-comprehensive efforts as an urgent task took precedence over transformational goals. Fresno Unified School District was faltering and at risk of a state takeover. Members of that group and others convinced the school board a new superintendent was necessary because the incumbent was not equipped to be a change agent in our community. Dr. Walt Buster, a CRI member and former superintendent of a neighboring school district, volunteered to step in. His offer was accepted on a

5-2 vote of the school board and he recruited a small planning team to craft a bow-to-stern turn-around plan. Its primary author, Pete Weber, a retired Fortune 500 company executive, coined the term "Focused Blitzkrieg," as the only way to fundamentally change direction. Weber's assessment of the school district: "Everything that needed to be uniform was random and everything that needed to be customized was locked down tight." Weber's quick-change approach was not only essential but also realistic as the "CEO function" for the effort included someone seasoned in leading large operations and turnarounds. In transformation work, a CEO function is a seamless *team* of high-level people committed solely to the ultimate, community outcome, even if one member may be more visible than others working behind the scenes.

The school district intervention may well be one of the most important actions in which the FBC participated. The community's largest human-development system was hemorrhaging kids and leaving them with limited life choices – dependency, marginal employment or gangs. The huge numbers of under-developed people in Fresno and the problems they created were no match for government, nonprofit and faith-based efforts. Without the intervention, our community destiny would remain an economy built upon government services, taxes and grants. In that scenario, our residents would continue to struggle with poor health, poverty, crime and limited educational achievement.

Instead, the transition involved difficult negotiations with unions and terminating people that the second interim superintendent knew were problematic. Changes set the stage for new leadership under Superintendent Michael Hanson, who has wholeheartedly embraced the challenge.

Hanson was attracted to Fresno by the community's willingness to take responsibility for its schools. No doubt there will be a future book about how to transform a troubled urban school district into a system that meets all children where they are and provides them with an opportunity to achieve their potential.

Chapter 6

WHAT LIES BENEATH

The shadow side of humanity and its traumatic impact can leave lasting marks on the psyche, preventing people from experiencing a fulfilling life. But we must recognize the darkness to be enlightened about the challenges we face in the San Joaquin Valley.

As a Minnesotan, my exposure to interventions and Twelve Step programs were many. The Minnesota Legislature meets part time, so when it was out of session I worked for Community Intervention, which taught communities across the country about addiction, intervention and recovery using schools as the central hub for effective action. As an attorney handling criminal cases, I came to realize that by the time clients got to me their fate was pretty well cast. Most grew up with addicts, became addicts and helped develop future addicts.

The Johnson Institute in Minneapolis was created to develop a model to attempt early interventions to raise "the bottom". Conventional wisdom held that alcoholics and other addicts must descend to despair losing everything before being motivated to recover. Herb Johnson thought otherwise, implementing the concept of early intervention that has saved individuals, families and communities from great suffering and huge social costs. While some joke that Minnesota is the land of 10,000 treatment centers or the state of compassion, its high rankings economically and socially are due largely to a culture based upon commitment to personal and collective responsibility and a norm of kindness.

In Fresno, I realized my Community Intervention experience would be a potent tool, with individuals and families, but also in the community. A Minneapolis Police Department friend had urged me not to move to this region because it was a hub for drugs, contraband and gang members coming to the United States from South and Central America. Having been trained in the field of addictions, it was alarming to identify many practicing addicts held important positions in the community. Addiction is a health issue and an adaptive survival tool, so I've learned not to condemn or judge people, while holding them accountable for behavior.

One could argue that addiction and many other seemingly dysfunctional behaviors make sense from the perspective of a survivor, but I am always cautious about the perceptions and thinking of an active addict and will not support them in their desire for positions of trust and power. Active addicts can also be poor team members as self-absorption is typically a central feature.

Most think of alcohol and drug addiction, yet two of the most damaging addictions are to power and sex. Others include food, video gaming, gambling, shopping, nicotine, work and caffeine. Author Ann Wilson Schaef long ago prophesied that addiction would become normal in our culture and that communities must confront it to recover and thrive.

My sense is addictions are variations of materialism. For some it's an insatiable desire for more of whatever creates a buzz. For others, it's based upon a desperate need not to feel the hopelessness, pain and fear lying beneath the urge to use. While addiction is complex and multidimensional, fundamentally it is about looking for solutions on the outside that can only be found within and in a trusted community.

Neuroscientists continue to significantly deepen our understanding of causation and recovery from this terrible plague.

Our founders created a country based upon the belief that we all have intrinsic value and could govern ourselves. Pursuit of happiness has as much to do with achieving self-mastery and a life of integrity as it does achieving external goals. A quality life consists of inner and outer as reflections of each another. Addiction prevents this.

Ensuring that everyone has this opportunity to reach full potential is in our personal and collective self-interest. Lives of quiet desperation and acts of deliberate harm or unconscious destruction are symptoms of the failure to do the difficult inner work of self-discovery or the lack of opportunity to do so. Teaching people how to do this work is critical to sustaining a healthy culture and preserving freedom, rather than defaulting into the easier exploitation and dependence.

My professional work in Minnesota prepared me well for my job in Fresno. Because the culture of Minnesota is community oriented, good government approaches were considered common sense. However, I was keenly aware this was not the case in most other states or in Congress, where single interests and money have always threatened good public policy. My work at both Common Cause and Community Intervention helped me see that individuals within an unhealthy, highly competitive culture can reduce people to objects, core values to numbers and the environment into a dump or resource colony.

At Community Intervention workshops, we taught that in dysfunctional families, the members assume roles and develop survival skills – including addiction – to endure the pain, chaos and isolation. In my experience, the family heroes are the most likely to enter the corporate world or other highly competitive endeavors because their strengths are a very strong work ethic and often a desire to provide for others. These traits can become problematic when narrow goals are pursued without considering the impact on other issues. For instance, lowering costs can lead to lower quality, wages that cannot sustain a family or to environmental impacts that cause significant damage over time.

The family system model can be useful at the macro level to explore society as a whole. Other family roles include the scapegoat, lost child, mascot, enabler and primary addict. The scapegoat is typically the patient, the person blamed for the family problems. If we look at the poor as the scapegoat of the system, we can look to culture and the environment rather than just point to individual behavior, which is how public health professionals look at solutions. They don't just focus on getting individuals to change; they try to create conditions making healthy choices easier than maladaptive behaviors.

Lost children learn to be invisible, hoping they won't be hit, yelled at or ridiculed. How many lost children sat silently as colleagues sold mortgages they knew wouldn't be paid back or products they knew were defective or harmful? How many watched as fellow teachers treated children with challenges as inferior beings? How many enablers make excuses for unacceptable behavior or hide the evidence after misdeeds are done at home or work? Broken families equate to a broken society desperately needing transformational approaches to turn the tide and heal our culture.

Those born to wealth are often disconnected from the labor and risk it took to create great fortunes. As former Texas Gov. Ann Richards said, "They were born on third and thought they hit a triple." Rather than discover their gifts and test their mettle, some heirs choose a life of comfort, and then pass it down to the next generation, diluting – even extinguishing – the passion that created a business thus putting it at risk. When legacy rather than merit-based leadership predominates, the community is at risk of deterioration.

At the root of so many of our challenges is failure to complete the concept of capitalism to ensure that everyone has an opportunity to pursue happiness.

The economy is a system of overlapping buckets. Those able and inspired to consistently pursue excellence and growth are suited to larger enterprises and global competition, while many are satisfied with midsize, regional operations offering goods and services based upon customized needs and assets of a given geography. Some are interested in running small local businesses and others are drawn to cooperatives, social businesses and nonprofits, whose value may be best measured in dollars saved and quality of life created, rather than dollars produced. Another bucket holds professionals, artisans and artists who develop an expertise, trade or passion that provides their livelihood. And there are those with significant mental, physical or emotional limitations who may need some form of sheltered workshop to be fully engaged.

As Freud explained, work and love are the foundation of mental health. Contribution and connection provide the web of community and the roots of individual sanity. It is in everyone's best interest that all residents have both the opportunity and support to live their best life. We need all elements of the economy functioning well and leveraging one another. When one component dominates, the ecosystem is thrown out of whack and ultimately everyone's quality of life suffers. Bigger, faster, more cultures with only a single bottom line as the driver have grown like a brain tumor that destroys the healthy cells and ultimately kills the host.

While this "empire orientation" phenomenon is international, the consequences are concentrated in the poorer regions which are seen as resources to be exploited, not intrinsically valuable. Some see this as addiction, with money and power likened to habit-forming crack cocaine. Major business publications have labeled CEOs of some corporations psychopaths. When value is reduced to numbers and the pressure is on, people react. Teachers and students may cheat in the face of high-stakes testing or stockholders may demand profits every quarter, for example. We can fault the people who play the game or examine the ecosystem that tempts them. How many corporations that we condemn offer stocks we hold within the mutual funds of our own retirement portfolios? Blame is a distraction, and deep understanding that leads to effective response is the path forward.

Chapter 7

THROUGH THE ECONOMIC SPYGLASS

A lot had been accomplished through the Collaborative Regional Initiative, including 26 projects launched and many completed. Support from the James Irvine Foundation gave us the resources to convene a second community leader retreat in Monterey. Some in the group had been involved since the beginning; others were new to the effort. Besides evaluating progress, a critical component was renewal and envisioning what would be next. This process yielded two very important projects accompanied by an understanding of their interdependence.

We selected reading proficiently by third grade as No. 1 priority. Based upon this decision, Kurt Madden led the effort to create ReadFresno, originally conceived as an effort to align existing reading programs and to fill gaps.

As job creation was the No. 2 priority, seeds were planted for the Regional Jobs Initiative (RJI) and what would become a five-year, comprehensive economic development strategy. While it began as a special initiative, a collaborative culture has continued to evolve as a result of the CRI and RJI. It is becoming standard operating procedure for economic development and other efforts.

The Regional Jobs Initiative was the product of a recommendation from the *Meeting the Challenge* report commissioned by Fresno Mayor

Alan Autry for the city and the CRI. The report underscored the relationship between a weak economy and high costs of law enforcement and social problems. While the path to transformation remained unclear, recognizing that changes in the economy were essential to solving social problems had become indisputable in the minds of many.

The RJI subsumed most of the remaining projects of the CRI and its value based operating system. The RJI cultivated some strong clusters, particularly in water technology; offered important lessons in how to get things done; and developed cross-sector relationships. However, it also distracted from the larger picture of the community as a whole.

While improving the economy was a top priority, the lens through which planning and actions are taken is vitally important. Working harder, but using the same game board, was not going to reach root causes of poverty. Playing Monopoly better, rather than creating a new game aimed at achieving an abundant community, was unlikely to change the demographics of the region.

While we learned a lot through the RJI effort and important aspects of it continue, our thinking began at the level of economic development, not stewardship as we understand it today. Transformation demanded we go deeper and higher to better understand how the overall community economy worked and its implications at all levels.

Chapter 8

BLAMING THE VICTIM VS.
UNDERSTANDING THE CONTEXT

Every year we learn more about the evolution and depth of the San Joaquin Valley's poverty. There is a longstanding lack of funding parity from the state and national governments in key systems and infrastructure. Also, there are low levels of philanthropic investment locally and from state and national foundations. The lack of large corporate headquarters removes another common source of significant funding and high-level talent available elsewhere.

Decisions in areas as far ranging as immigration, the Farm Bill, welfare, education and health, and even where to locate refugees from the Vietnam War played roles in concentrating poverty in the San Joaquin Valley. Other regions gave newly released prisoners bus passes to Fresno. Foster-care operators purchased low-cost homes in Fresno, adding children with significant challenges to the local school system. The region's low living costs and temperate weather attracted others with limited skills.

Our region has been called the "Appalachia of the West" and "the new Ellis Island." Reading the inscription on the Statue of Liberty, there is a certain haunting sense of history in what has emerged in our region. What have we forgotten? How could we have allowed conditions rivaling Third World poverty to lodge amidst our great wealth? Emma Lazarus' poem at the base of the statue expresses the sense of desperation of those escaping terrible conditions and the welcoming grace of those with resources in a brave new world. Those that flee poverty, religious persecution or political oppression bring with them a resiliency and resolve in their DNA that renews and challenges us.

> *Not like the brazen giant of Greek fame,*
> *With conquering limbs astride from land to land;*
> *Here at our sea-washed, sunset gates shall stand*
> *A mighty woman with a torch, whose flame*
> *Is the imprisoned lightning, and her name*
> *Mother of Exiles. From her beacon-hand*
> *Glows worldwide welcome; her mild eyes command*
> *The air-bridged harbor that twin cities frame.*
>
> *"Keep, ancient lands, your storied pomp!" cries she*
> *with silent lips. "Give me your tired, your poor,*
> *Your huddled masses yearning to breathe free,*
> *The wretched refuse of your teeming shore.*
> *Send these, the homeless, tempest-tost to me,*
> *I lift my lamp beside the golden door!"*
> **Emma Lazarus**, *The New Colossus*

The Colossus of Rhodes, one of the Seven Wonders of the Ancient World, offers an interesting contrast to the thrust of the poem. Where the original was a man, an enormous statue constructed to celebrate Rhodes' victory over the ruler of Cyprus, *The New Colossus* offers a different message embracing acceptance and equity.

With political and social boundaries in flux and economic and health impacts felt globally, figuring out how to frame issues related to resources and survival will continue to challenge everyone. Fresno, with its extremes and archetypes, offers an excellent opportunity to experiment and hopefully resolve these difficult paradoxes by leveraging our strengths to achieve community transformation.

The Rockefeller Foundation has been studying other regions in the United States with similar conditions – Appalachia, the Deep South and the Rio Grande Valley. The conclusion: When a single, dominant industry controls economic opportunity and the middle class is employed by this industry, government or in poverty remediation efforts, the strengths of the middle class are weakened. The middle class tends to band together to tackle community problems and maintain a bridge to connect the upper and lower classes. This group values the opportunity for socio-economic movement through hard work and education – the American Dream. Without a vibrant middle class, polarities between classes expand and the forces of greed and need can unleash fear and the damaging attitudes of privilege and entitlement.

When I moved to Fresno, I was perplexed that we were in the heart of the most productive agricultural region in the world yet people went hungry and ate junk food because that was all they had available. Unknown to me were the notions of food desert, where no healthy food is available, and food swamp, where fast junk food is all around.

In Minnesota, there were retail food co-ops, but surprisingly none in Fresno. That's when I understood the practical implications of the missing link: Without a vital middle class, there is no heart of the community from which to stand and work together.

As the Rockefeller Foundation learned, the primary issue is not race, but the lack of economic opportunity that is generative rather than dependent upon the dominant industry or its shadow. While not meant to ignore the unique and crushing impact of slavery or racism, this insight points to shared economic causation and a path forward.

Big government, scarcity-minded nonprofits and anti-business equity advocates could be considered the symptoms of a Monopoly economy. When I did some research on the thinking behind this popular game I learned the goal was not simply to grow rich, what I thought, but to also bankrupt everyone else. The solution is not to fight Goliath. At one point he was an entrepreneur struggling to survive, too. The solution is to complete the economy with other industries, innovative and collaborative business models and a wide mix of educational pathways.

Where poverty has become chronic, systemic and endemic, serious attention must also be paid to values and internal human development. A victim consciousness is often festering inside those who suffer from oppression and defeat. Ironically, the same fear is often hosted inside those committed to the status quo because they fear the loss of their position, privilege or wealth. People who grow up dependent or as legacies of great riches often lack both the mindset and the skills to fend for themselves. The greater the gap between rich and poor, the more likely it is that people will polarize rather than work together to solve problems and ensure opportunity.

Wrote author and evangelist Jim Wallis:

"Corporate CEOs, no less than everyone else, have a responsibility to the common good, not just to the bottom line. The entrepreneurial spirit and social innovation fostered by a market economy has benefitted many and should not be overly encumbered by unnecessary or stifling regulations. But left to its own devices and human weakness, the market will too often disintegrate into greed and corruption. Capitalism needs rules, or it easily becomes destructive. A healthy, balanced relationship between free enterprise, on the one hand, and public accountability and regulation, on the other is morally and practically essential."

Chapter 9

THE GIANT SEA ANCHOR

I remember a sinking feeling when I came to Fresno and my husband said, "I can't live here. There are too many poor people and there is too much pain."

I sensed initially – and continue to believe – that Fresno's biggest challenge is within. The culture and material poverty are symptoms of a belief system based upon scarcity, inadequacy and fear concentrated in the minds of residents.

It wasn't until 2006, when a major conference put on by the California Endowment exposed the depth and breadth of the poverty we faced, that we finally reach a tipping point. *Worlds Apart; Futures Together* was attended by people from all sectors and socio-economic groups. It offered an important step toward unity as we heard that Fresno, not New Orleans or Appalachia, had the most concentrated urban poverty in America and our rural communities were in even worse shape. A Brookings Institution report, released after images of Hurricane Katrina's impact were burned into our minds, contrasted our situation with other communities. The reality of our circumstances was sobering and also catalyzed action.

Ken Newby, managing partner of Deloitte/Fresno, became a champion for raising what he calls "the giant sea anchor of poverty." In addition to the moral implications, he realized that if we did not do so we would never achieve the economic prosperity and community betterment we sought.

Moralizing, government programs, faith-based efforts or advocacy alone cannot solve the problem of poverty. It requires the skills, influence and resources of the private sector. As we have learned through global poverty remediation efforts, solutions are to be found in microloans, trade, new business models, education, and financial literacy. They are found through authentic relationship and humility, working with not for or at someone who may be much scrappier and intelligent that the person with the helping hand. While it can be comforting to think we made it on our own, a deeper look reveals we all stand on the shoulders of others.

Programs that simply address survival needs are important, but alone can be insufficient and often damaging. Solutions to poverty are internal and external and must be advanced simultaneously beginning with those who are ready. Failing to execute these approaches means government will react and build prisons, increase law enforcement, expand social services and chase after the symptoms of poverty, including poor health, addiction and low educational achievement.

"For every talent that poverty has stimulated it has blighted a hundred."
John W. Gardner

The *Human Investment Initiative* is a comprehensive transformation strategy to address human development targeting both neighborhoods of concentrated poverty and traditional approaches to education, health and justice systems. Oppressive material poverty is one of many barriers to the full expression of an individual's potential. The plan integrated our diverse professional training and multidisciplinary research into a package of strategies based upon a new mindset. Released in 2008 with significant support from the Fresno Regional Foundation, the report generated passionate responses, both positive and negative. Because it was aimed at systemic transformation, not symptom relief, funders caught up in measuring tactical approaches were not interested.

One of the fiercest objections was raised by a long time anti-poverty leader, angry not at the content; but rather at the source of the document, a business group. He believed poverty was caused by business. He was expressing what the Rockefeller Foundation had discovered about dominant, low-cost industries. His solution was more programs, not job creation. For years government programs were probably the only solution available as many people had accepted chronic poverty as inevitable in the region.

While the *Human Investment Initiative* did not move forward as a complete package, elements have advanced, including the Bridge Academy, to align government programs in a central location. The settlement houses of the past were based upon this concept of a one-stop shop where people with limited resources could be equipped for living-wage employment. Another issue that is advancing is mental health, which will be highlighted in a later chapter. Other components involving health, justice and education are continuing to evolve. Most importantly, as we have learned more about how to apply the strengths of capitalism to urban poverty, our strategies have become more holistic and more broadly supported.

We have learned that you cannot transform the human development sphere from within any more than we could transform economic development in isolation. Transformation eliminates the conditions that give rise to the behavior and mindset we seek to change. Unless we address the underlying conditions, the result is a set of disconnected, expensive and often competing industrial complexes aimed at health, education and justice.

Remediation and control are very expensive and the antithesis of personal responsibility and freedom. These qualities are the result of inner development in terms of character and self-knowledge alongside the external development of marketable skills. By creating supportive environments, more people will have the opportunity to develop their potential and all will benefit from their gifts.

Strategies for changing the conditions are most likely to be found at higher level of thinking that sees interdependence of all the sectors and can identify the leveraging points – the Fourth Sphere, as we call it. It is a lens wide and round enough to view the whole community, so we can discover assets and resources that are invisible from within a silo, discipline or sector. Many of our most intractable issues are not anyone's responsibility; they are everyone's. While organizations and institutions may be obligated to treat the symptoms, eliminating underlying conditions and primary prevention require community-wide engagement.

Solutions require customized local strategies along with aligned investments along the vertical axis from private, government and foundation sources. While this can be view negatively as "top down", when it comes to execution without alignment and accountability outcomes remains elusive. Collective action at the bottom is prevented or marginal when those at the top aren't thinking and acting together. This failure of high level alignment often results in impermeable, wasteful, costly, redundant siloes and conflicting regulations. Nobody wins yet we tend to blame those working the hardest, those on the frontlines doing the heroic daily bailing in a leaky, mindless system.

Chapter 10

FOCUSED BLITZKRIEG

What do the Internet, Alcoholics Anonymous and VISA International have in common with the promise of democracy? Quite a bit, they're:

- Nearly ubiquitous.
- Spread through attraction not promotion because they effectively meet authentic needs.
- Sustained without central control.
- Not owned by anyone.
- Chaordic organizations that are self-organizing and self-governing. (Dee Hock, the founder of VISA, coined the word to integrate the forces of chaos and order.)
- Operating through networks of voluntary participants who benefit from the interaction, not through hierarchies of authority.
- Common purpose, ethical operating principles and responsibility distributed through every node make them work, not power or coercion.

Recognizing that the economy, the built and natural environment and social issues are interdependent challenges us to find ways to think through the implications and act accordingly. This can be a difficult and lengthy process. As noted earlier, when we started Fresno's Collaborative Regional Initiative in 2000, we used a Venn diagram that illustrated how the economy, the environment and equity overlapped in very obvious and not so obvious ways. As we continued our attempts

41

to implement this concept, we discovered the cultures, players and goals of the different spheres were often at odds and all operated at vastly different speeds.

Economic factors move fast. Being first to market could mean life or death. High-stakes competition is endemic and disruptive innovation is ongoing.

The infrastructure sphere – buildings, roads, bridges of the built environment – is largely the province of government, requiring huge financial resources and long timelines. Glacial comes to mind. The natural environment is considered sacred by activists and preservation in its most pristine form is paramount. Economic forces may see the natural environment as a resource to be exploited. Land is valued at its most profitable use, so it's easy to understand how those committed to the natural environment are often at loggerheads with those who want to create jobs and develop profitable businesses.

When you add the human element and the impact on residents is factored into economic and environmental sphere decisions, the best path forward is even more complex. Those living in prosperous regions can righteously champion environmental concerns, while those living amid high poverty simply want the quality jobs that manufacturing can bring.

Deeply understanding the inter-relationships among the spheres and then making wise, sustainable decisions requires discipline, due diligence and a steward's perspective. We definitely talked the talk before beginning to take steps along an integrated path where impacts on all three spheres were included at the vision and planning stages. Steward leadership is a developmental process.

To hold the spheres together visually and intentionally, we came up with the Fourth Sphere framework. It offers a platform where citizens can stand together as equals to participate in the reflective dialogue necessary to move beyond stakeholder interests to community solutions. It clarifies the necessary elements to make the Fourth Sphere effective.

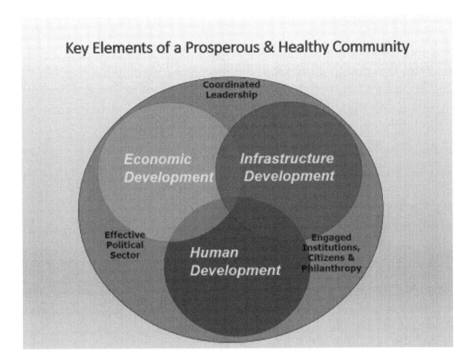

Key Elements of a Prosperous & Healthy Community

The Fourth Sphere is an answer to Einstein's teaching, "You cannot solve a problem at the level of thinking that created it." Another quote is even more intriguing, "Intellectuals solve problems, geniuses prevent them." This could be understood as experts focus on what they know, innovators are impartial and imagine possibilities. They know they don't know. Blank sheets of paper are their happy place.

When stakeholders try to reach consensus, the thinking typically begins at what's in it for me and proceeds toward the short-term benefits for a few. In contrast, wisdom favors excellence, finding the best answer and considering the future.

In ideal configuration, pillars of the Fourth Sphere include an effective political sector, engaged citizens, institutions and enlightened philanthropy. Coordinated leadership – stewardship of the whole – would be the new way to conduct the community's business and could be applied to any challenge that required community-wide collaboration, including a library tax or school bond.

The Fourth Sphere offers an opportunity to demonstrate the truth of "United we stand; divided we fall" vs. the folly of fragmentation and chaos. When the public as a whole has no voice and elected officials hear only from single, often well-funded interests, we can't be surprised that decisions go to the highest bidder or loudest voices.

When John W. Gardner founded Common Cause in 1970, the inciting battle cry was "Everybody is organized except the people." However, serving this organization taught me that good government processes and campaign finance reforms are not enough. Our toughest issues today cross every boundary and discipline. Relying on experts is risky. They often find a way to fit the messy reality of life into a tidy model they developed through their limited frame of expertise and experiences. Most solutions require elements of all the three primary spheres.

While consultants and academics often have promising theories, few have experienced the sweat, tears and perseverance it takes to execute with real people on the ground where change actually happens. Too often, those at the top are disembodied heads that change schemes before the last one has made it through a system creating a whiplash that leads to simply waiting out new leaders, bureaucratic inertia, or despair. The Fourth Sphere, however, offers a platform where the strengths of these elements can be tapped, but the leadership and commitment is sustained by the people most affected by the results – a community's residents and taxpayers.

Lately, there seems to be great angst between top-down and bottom-up approaches to solutions – a natural reaction to the years of strategies created by "outside" experts and imposed without sufficient insights of those directly affected. This approach is particularly ineffective applied to human development.

Filling out a form differently, retooling a machine part, even changing a "fact" can be an easy change, although there are many who still believe Pluto is a regular planet. However, anyone who has tried to get someone to change behavior or learn something new – stop drinking, start exercising, learn to read, face fears – knows how futile outside pressure can be.

Readiness, strong desire and willingness to persevere in the face of setbacks, is personal, unpredictable and essential. It has been easier to simply treat symptoms of human failure rather than transform underlying conditions that crushed motivations in the first place. This challenge requires cultural change considered by many to be the toughest leadership task of all. I suspect this what Einstein was encouraging us to do. Change the level of thinking.

Thinking and acting in silos, rather than addressing root causes, we built huge industrial complexes to treat symptoms in justice, health and social services. While we all know that "an ounce of prevention is worth a pound of cure," we did not have a platform to advance comprehensive, integrated strategies. Instead, the costly industrial complexes continued to grow, became increasingly symbiotic and funneled tax dollars down endless pipes leading nowhere. Even worse: Too many caught up in these systems continued to deteriorate and suffer while passing their dysfunction on to their children.

When an economy is based primarily on a single bottom line, externalizing costs and securing single-interest subsidies is simply part of the game. When the job continuum started to dry up as large corporations sent jobs offshore, mechanization and technology eliminated others and bigger was considered better, we lost sight of what is needed for balance and community vibrancy.

Bigger, if value-based, *can* be better, but too often is just greed. Becoming big can result in anonymity, severing a personal connection to others. Deciding to lay people off, send jobs to other countries and bring harmful products to market is all too easy if you don't see the faces of those bearing the personal costs of these decisions. I remember the power of Al Gore saying that his father stopped growing tobacco after his sister died of lung cancer.

What do we do once we know we are off course? A physician friend told me the chemists who came up with high-fructose corn syrup probably thought they were doing a good thing. I wonder if those who produce or market highly sweetened, denatured breakfast cereal to children will stop when their own children become obese or develop diabetes.

Big often makes adapting to new truths difficult. Truth upsets business models and can lower profits. When big means Congressional or legislative influence that results in continued subsidies for what causes harm and derails innovation, we all eventually lose.

When a business, nonprofit, church or even a person is more concerned with survival than its original mission, it can start living backwards, from the outside in. Acting like cancer, rather than an essential player in a healthy ecosystem, a self-absorbed cell will multiply and eventually kill the host. Narcissism is a particularly virulent form of insanity. Indeed, over the long term it is a form of suicide.

Based upon what we learned in Fresno after more than a decade of study and action, we began to build a platform with a governance approach that included leaders from all our spheres. As thinking from the Fourth Sphere is new and challenging for most, developing tools for teaching this skill has been a high priority. No one has given more thought or provided deeper insights into what we have learned than Ken Newby, a Certified Public Accountant.

His high-level professional experience, innate curiosity, intellectual courage, and ability to synthesize provided us with numerous documents, Power Points and other tools to make complexity more user-friendly. I learned painfully at Common Cause that "being right is the booby prize." If nothing happens because people cannot understand, it doesn't matter.

Teaching what we have learned, through repeated exposure and application, is an important element of this work and its sustainability and we are at the early stages. The Tips and Tools section presents specific applications and materials that help us share what we have learned.

As the Fresno Business Council board has representatives from all sectors, we offer a holistic environment to incubate and lead stewardship initiatives. This platform for action is new civic infrastructure. A number of core initiatives have been launched from this platform. Recognizing that we have to sustain "legitimate authority," while maintaining an entrepreneurial spirit to have impact and create a new normal, it essential that the top leaders of key institutions remain engaged.

All of our institutions' successes are hampered by scarce resources and the many symptoms of chronic poverty. Yet, acting alone, none have the authority or resources to address either underlying conditions or the most troubling challenges – a mental health crisis, high crime and deplorable levels of child abuse and neglect. By teaming up, they can become managing partners of the community together.

Those willing to lead and learn amid the ambiguity of a start-up are a very small subset of the population. Just like our barn-raising forebears, we don't need a lot of paid people to do the work of the community, and it can be counterproductive. This is the work of citizens. The price of freedom. However, we do need a handful with special skills, a certain temperament and time. We need people who are able to hold the vision, remain impartial, have high-level peacemaking skills, communicate skillfully and stay committed to personal growth. The era of complexity requires stewards to have a working knowledge of multiple disciplines, be lifelong learners and find satisfaction in developing others, as well as being the change themselves.

A great community is adaptive, resilient, confident, wise and inclusive. When leaders and citizens have these attributes, prosperity, peace and wellbeing are the likely outcomes. The test of sustainability is what happens when these leaders move on and are replaced. Because executing the stewardship initiatives will involve the resources and, in some cases, policies of various institutions, leadership changes create a time of risk. By its nature, transformational work is multi-generational and requires deep commitment. Too often the work is reduced to a method or model and the history and impetus for its creation are forgotten as has happened with America.

A high priority for the Fresno Business Council is creating a pipeline and providing ongoing reminders of the responsibilities of citizenship. "The price of freedom is eternal vigilance" and variations of this seminal quote have been attributed several founding fathers. Laurels, entitlements and privilege are all defenses against profound acceptance of the fact Heraclitus expressed as "All is flux; nothing says still."

Can we learn to respond confidently and effectively to changing conditions, new knowledge and lessons learned or will we fearfully and ineffectually try to control, manipulate or simply deny what is happening around us? Can we recover from faster, bigger, more and create a more natural, sustainable rhythm and a culture that nurtures and restores, rather than stresses and fragments? These are choices every individual and community must make. The answers quite likely rest upon what cultural leaders decide.

Chapter 11

PASSING THE TORCH

"The longer I live, the more I respect enthusiasm. There is no perfection of technique that will substitute for the lift of spirit that enthusiasm produces. Some people keep their zest until the day they die. They keep their sense of curiosity. They reach out. They enjoy. They risk failure. They may even allow themselves some moderately cheerful expectations for the time ahead. Such expectations may be greeted with skepticism in the current climate, but we should welcome the buoyance from which they spring. Otherwise, in our world weary wisdom, we shall be unresponsive to the challenges that keep societies alive and moving."
John W. Gardner

There are countless books on leadership and stewardship, even some on followership. Many have inspired me, given me insights or taught skills. I am a lifelong student of John W. Gardner, considered by many to be one of America's greatest citizens and philosophers. His timeless books have had the greatest impact on me.

As I hit the inevitable bumps along the way, despairing that we would never achieve our goals, I would pick up one of his books and be renewed. He wrote extensively about America and its traditions in *On Leadership, Self-Renewal and The Innovative Society, Excellence—Can We Be Equal and Excellent, Too?* and *Morale.*

If you are not inclined to read them all, Gardner, his daughter and PBS commentator Bill Moyers created the compendium *Living, Leading and the American Dream.* It captures the essence of Gardner's work, his passion for the ideals of our country, and his belief that as citizens we would remember our responsibilities as a free and brave people and continue to work toward a just and civil society.

If I were to design curriculum for junior high, I would embed these books into civics and history classes when our brain basically reboots and our sense of self changes making us more open to outside influences. Puberty also is when hormones kick in, creating internal chaos. We don't honor this tumultuous time with a Vision Quest and nurturing support as indigenous people did to help their children retain internal identity and discern a sense of purpose. No, we uproot our children from their grade schools and toss them into what for many feels like a giant warehouse – junior high, letting them fend for themselves in a *Lord of the Flies* experience where many learn the painful lessons of survival of the fittest.

Imagine if we taught our children at this vulnerable time about the importance of self-mastery, self-actualization and the goals they can pursue unlimited by circumstances of their birth because others sacrificed to make it so. We could provide our teens with the tools of self-reflection they could use for a lifetime and teach them how to create a life of purpose and contribution. We could include Dr. James Comer's brilliant work on child development and, while they still had adult supervision, teach children how to create a just and civil society. We could include the innovative work of John McKnight and Peter Block, who's recent *The Abundant Community – Awakening the Power of Families and Neighborhoods* eloquently reminds us that everyone has a gift and an important contribution to make.

Our collective challenge is to ensure that we create environments where everyone has the opportunity to develop their gifts and earn a living by sharing them. A deeper, more-difficult challenge is instilling within the participants the enduring motivation to succeed and the importance of feeling part of the whole.

Without intentional guidance, a deep understanding of America's purpose, and an opportunity to practice in a safe environment, many children don't develop a sense of gratitude and or inspiration from the American story. Without that, they are unlikely to develop into great citizens.

Self-absorption and greed, in psychological terms, can be labeled as narcissism and addiction. Entitlement and dependency are the ensnaring traps we created in lieu of relationship building and changing underlying conditions. The political polarities that have emerged regarding poverty, blend ignorance with denial as each side focuses on half of the problem and half of the solution, leaving those stuck in poverty at an impasse.

In a culture obsessed with bigger, more, and faster we have made celebrities – even role models – of folks addled by greed and narcissism. We need to learn to cheer for the elite in every field and come to realize that an excellent hospice worker has every bit as much value as a corporate Titan, movie star or Olympic athlete. Time and context have a way of teaching us things we don't want to know.

American swimmer Michael Phelps offered a terrific example of the paradox of striving for personal excellence and being a friend and member of the team. When his friend beat him, Phelps acknowledged his disappointment, cheered his friend's victory and led the American Olympic team as an equal, albeit obvious leader, answering Gardner's question: "Can we be excellent and equal too?"

We are all challenged to strive for personal excellence while cheering on those around us.

Many of the people involved in transformational work around the country were mentored by Gardner or found others who inspired them. There will always be those who are outliers in every generation, those who are so smitten with the ideals of America they spend their lives working to manifest the original vision.

However, outliers are not enough. They are too easily dismissed as naïve, zealots or crazy. We must focus on the culture itself and make the responsibilities of citizenship and stewardship normal. Changing culture can seem like an impossible task. Yet, Roger Bannister broke the 4-minute-mile "barrier" in 1954 when even medical experts said it was humanly impossible. Today the record is 17 seconds below, proving we can always do better if we simply decide to and persevere.

I believe the stewardship pipeline begins at home. Comer taught us that when it doesn't we must focus on child development and teach children how to create a just and civil society in our schools, or we can pay the price in lost contributions and desperate acts motivated by addiction, crime and self-destruction. Comer is a child psychiatrist at Yale who wrote *Leave No Child Beyond,* which was inspired by the call-to-arms issued by the Children's Defense Fund. This concept in America is typically associated with the Bush administration's education plan, but his initiative diverged greatly from the ideals espoused by the original thinking. Rather than a focus on standardized testing, the emphasis was on creating new school environments and meeting the developmental needs of deprived children that a healthy family would provide by osmosis.

While all parents should prepare their children for school and life, many don't know how, can't or won't. Many of those who corrupted our financial, corporate and civic institutions went to the best schools and were the children of privilege.

I have learned there is often little difference internally between those at the top and those at the bottom when they become addicts. *It's all about me* simply looks different when you wield a pen or computer rather than point a gun. I'm compelled to ask:

- Which group do you think bears the most responsibility for the underlying conditions in America that give rise to despair and desperation?

- Who has the skills, influence, and resources to develop systems and environments that can achieve transformational change?
- How do we create a platform that will attract our best and brightest?
- How do we create enough trust in our leaders to make the tough decisions needed to change direction?
- How do we let go of our narrow perspectives and step back to see the whole where we will be able to see the paradoxes clearly and realize our presumed enemies may actually be our allies?

Most of us want the same things. We just need see the whole picture and integrate differences at a higher level of thinking so we're able to do what appears impossible. Developing a stewardship pipeline must become a multifaceted endeavor with targets and strategies for all ages. Stewards are everywhere and others aspire to become so. However, most don't know the community business because they are put off by politics and politicians. They may focus on a particular issue and invest time and treasure trying to make a difference only in a narrow space.

Fragmented efforts may temporarily alleviate symptoms, but they don't achieve transformational change. Thinking of stewards and citizens interchangeably – people who take responsibility for their communities – it is essential that we put stewards in leadership positions. Stewards in this context have positions of authority through election, appointment or a hiring process and also a deep understanding of themselves, the mission of their organization, and how it fits into the bigger picture. Those simply out for themselves or with narrow agendas do not bring out the best in others and are likely to do great damage to an institution, an organization, or a community entrusted to them. We have a choice about whom we follow. Followers have much more power than most realize. In most cases those who stand by and could have done something allow incompetent people to lead resulting in bad outcomes.

Key aspects of our efforts are workshops and other materials to teach the complexity of community business and develop the tools needed to apply the model. We intend to offer experiential learning and fellowships to cultivate leaders who stand on principles when there is something to lose, explore new paths when old maps no longer suit, and are more concerned with the enterprise's success than personal credit or power. It won't be a formal leadership program because this sort of leadership is best taught through inspiration, living examples, and through the words and deeds of those who have become stewards.

Chapter 12
HERE'S LOOKING AT YOU, KID.

Those of you who made it through *The Lord of the Flies* experience un-harmed – or missed it entirely – probably went on to lead productive, contributing lives and may wonder why others seem so troubled and stuck. Why can't they just snap out of it, tough it out or pick themselves up and move out of the wilderness of addiction, quiet desperation or shallow reflection where they lost their way? From your experience, people mired in poverty or lost in addictions may seem like foreigners who make no sense. Perhaps it's easier to dismiss their circumstances as their own fault rather than to challenge your thinking and be open to another perspective.

For much of my life, I thought I was one of you. Growing up mid-dle and then upper middle class in a small Wisconsin city and then the Twin Cities of Minnesota, my life seemed pretty traditional. I had good teachers and graduated with a BA in philosophy from the University of Minnesota and earned a JD from William Mitchell College of Law. I hit a bump in my law practice that changed everything personally and professionally.

I offer the information because it explains why I have some under-standing of those with difficult lives, those often cast as family scape-goats. While my story pales in comparison to comrades I have met along the recovery path, my experiences did help me develop a *bilin-gual* perspective. I'm fluent in the languages of victim and creator and of hero and scapegoat. I learned that whichever orientation dominates our life will determine both its quality and content.

Describing stewards as those who have done their inner work, or never had to if such souls exist, can mean different things. Some learned through osmosis growing up in a healthy family and others asked the hard questions about religion and life, finding answers about purpose and their relationship to others. Some were never the same after military service and those with a trauma history often stumble into introspection when their denial or survival skills no longer work. I fall into the last category, but had no idea until I was 26 and began to remember.

My legal career came to an abrupt end when I realized I could not find a way to practice law that did not compromise important values or was boring, and also that my inner world was a mess and I had to find a way to repair it. Both realities were revealed because of the acquittal of a man I believed was guilty of incest. I came up with the clever arguments that convinced the jury to let him off, sending two little girls home with a monster. My first reaction was to celebrate the victory because I no longer cared about justice; I just wanted to win. Then came a depth of self-loathing that drove me to despair and released memories buried so deep that I had no conscious recollection of them.

That fateful day I knew I would cease practicing law and find a way to heal. I realized that I had created an effective theory of defense from personal experience. Sexual abuse and rape were locked away in a Pandora's Box so deep within my psyche that I may never have known about them had it not been for that trial. Until this point, my external world looked pretty good, but it didn't match what was going on inside: Two people living in parallel universes.

To this day, I remain vigilant against those who try to control people with money as my perpetrator did. Dependence on someone else can translate into silence. Because my mother and other adults knew what was going on and did nothing to help, I am also committed to not being the person who remains mute when children are suffering or injustice abounds.

"*The hottest places in hell are reserved for those who, in times of great moral crisis, maintain their neutrality.*" Dante Alighieri

I was fortunate that I was living in Minnesota at the time of my awakening. The culture not only supports facing personal issues, it does so without judgment and offers a wide range of resources to help people heal. Many public leaders are open about their struggles. Some joke, "If you are not in recovery from something, we just figure you are in denial."

As more families have become dysfunctional, I suspect a higher percentage of people have become addicted to something: gambling, legal and illegal drugs, pornography, sex, work, caffeine, sugar, junk food and other behaviors and substances. There's a lot of money to be made from addicts and trauma survivors, so a broad and deep recovery in our country would spark many economic disruptions.

What I learned through my formal education cannot compare to what I learned about life and humanity through my healing journey. In sexual abuse boot camp I learned about some of the cruelest, most horrible acts adults inflict on children; how socio-economics often play a role; and that child cruelty occurs up and down the income continuum. I learned that many people can function in great pain and hold responsible positions even though terribly isolated and using a range of behaviors to cope and self-medicate. I learned that trauma knocks you off the grid. You can become disconnected from yourself and others. You live in fear. I also learned that the path to healing involves others and community.

While a long time coming, I also learned that the payoffs for the courage to heal are plentiful. While I found a way to recover and thank countless healers and friends who supported me in doing so, too many don't. They live in the shadows, just getting by and never finding the sense of inner peace or life satisfaction others enjoy. Sadly, too many find an "accidental" or direct way to commit suicide or they kill themselves in pieces through a lifetime of addiction or what can be labeled mental illness.

For a long time, I didn't feel comfortable either among those who are "normal" or those who are on an intentional healing journey. I rejected the victim label early when a wise counselor told me to reframe both the trauma and my survival strategies. She taught that the story is not as important as the priceless lessons. I am who I am. I could function and, due to my socio-economic upbringing, I seemed like everyone else. I could work and play alongside people who might be surprised by my history, but I would not risk telling them. When I did, though, many had their own stories to tell.

It is a sacred responsibility to speak for those who cannot. Grieving those who do not recover is a painful part of the journey. My closest friend in boot camp succeeded at suicide and others I dearly loved are also trail markers along the way. We all know that life is fragile. For the traumatized it is even more so.

What was known when I began recovery in the late 1970s and what we now know are, thankfully, worlds apart. Recent discoveries in neuroscience can lift us from polarized and unproductive thinking to transformational approaches that will result in substantial financial savings and relieve many from years of suffering.

"A bridge has no allegiance to either side." Les Coleman

Many people drawn to transformational work have had similar dramatic and catalytic events in their lives. While some people with a philosophical mindset are drawn to fundamental life questions such as who am I, why am I here and what is my relationship to others, most won't go there without prompting by cultural norms or an inciting incident. As part of regular education, we must encourage students to envision an outcome and figure out the pathway to get there. We cannot pursue happiness if we don't know who we are. If our goal in life is to fit in, comply with the rules or blindly believe what someone in authority told us is the truth, what is the point of freedom? How can we govern ourselves if we are uneducated about the world and our shared humanity?

Socrates was right, "The unexamined life is not worth living." However, unless people have their basic needs met and are encouraged to move along Maslow's hierarchy, this freedom is a luxury they cannot attain. A healthy democracy requires an educated, self-reflective and self-actualizing populace. We have the tools – public and private education. The root of education is the Greek word, *educare,* meaning to draw forth. The essence of the questioning Socratic Method is teaching children to think and to answer questions for themselves. Isn't that the essence of freedom?

PART TWO—TIPS AND TOOLS,
FRAMEWORKS AND APPLICATIONS

Chapter 13

GETTING DOWN TO IT—THINKING AND ACTING TOGETHER

The Scatter Diagram

The first thing you have to do to solve a problem is to understand it. But in our Nike-infused, "just do it" world the obvious is often the last thing we consider.

Action is heavily praised in our culture, while deep reflection is dismissed as inaction. The Fresno Business Council opted for action at the expense of learning and reflection when founding members bounced the retreat facilitator. They were confident that skills and approaches that had been successful at their own companies could be applied to community challenges. As a reinventing government specialist, the facilitator knew better, but was drowned out by the bluster of action-demanding voices.

The organization had to learn through experience that leading without authority is a new and vital skillset in any coalition of the willing. People in positions of power often have difficulty learning this new skill or acquiring the patience needed to earn trust *before* charging into action. Humility earned through failure typically signals that the lesson has been learned.

Business leaders, while essential, often fail when they take the helm of a government or community enterprise because confidential meetings and documents, quick decisions and holding others accountable are private-sector privileges. In the public realm, for the most part, they're a luxury. The community's business benefits from private-sector expertise. However its culture, processes and multiple bottom lines often are so frustrating to business people they give up. It is essential to think of everyone as a citizen first, to bring out the best in people. Each citizen is just one puzzle piece in the big picture, no larger or smaller than anyone else although some roles are interchangeable and others are not.

What's the problem? How we answer is critical, determining the actions we take and the successes we achieve. In the 6th century BCE, Chinese general and military strategist Sun Tzu taught us, "Tactics without strategy is the noise before defeat." He captures the frenzy of those who feel compelled to do something and focus on the most urgent, understandable problems. Crisis mentality may put out a few fires, but it stokes others if the underlying conditions of ignition are not changed. It is costly, exhausting and futile yet we've built huge industrial complexes aimed at symptoms.

Until we step back far enough to understand the problem, we will not align the resources needed to meet the challenge. Fortunately, as more people have understood that the "wicked messes" we face have many interdependent factors, innovative problem solving and leadership models are emerging.

After the *Worlds Apart; Futures Together* conference, Ken Newby started writing down the issues and conditions he heard during conversations about poverty and what to do about it. To help understand our problem, he created the scatter diagram, which has proven extremely useful in strategizing and in teaching how to do this work.

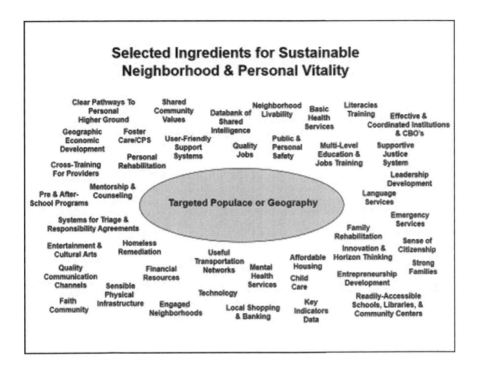

In the middle of the diagram he put the desired condition, such as "healthy neighborhood." Then he randomly circled it with a broad range of ingredients that would be necessary to make it so. One component of that neighborhood is children who develop into healthy, contributing adults. Clearly this is more likely if they're born to a healthy family, given quality food and guidance and exposed to diverse people and ideas. Unfortunately, many of Fresno's neighborhoods lack the positive ingredients and are scarred by negative ones.

Spelling out the ingredients necessary for a healthy neighborhood though the scatter diagram visually depicts why concentrated poverty is so difficult to remediate and can crush the spirit of the children living there. Upon entering school, some are already so far behind many never catch-up.

In addition to graphically explaining the problem, the scatter diagram also illustrates a critical point: No one institution, organization or sector has the responsibility, authority or resources to address all of the critical causal factors.

While some may be responsible for treating specific symptoms like crime, zoning violations or social supports, none can transform underlying conditions and offer the developmental pathways to lift both a neighborhood and people out of poverty. Public health approaches, where the primary focus is on the environment, are important, but without including an ongoing relational approach to the people and to community building, the odds of change are low.

Through the lens of the Fourth Sphere and concerted awareness of the other three, all sorts of possibilities and resources emerge to deploy against the scatter diagram. For instance Smart Growth, a holistic, long-term approach to development, accomplishes two goals – making the city financially healthier and cultivating better, more-prosperous neighborhoods as a result. Mixed use will bring back essential services and products while bringing economic development into the neighborhood. Multiple issues can be addressed simultaneously. Jobs can be created to fill food deserts and replace food swamps while also increasing incomes, building a stronger sense of community and improving health. Resources and programs devoted to entrepreneurial development and business start-ups can be aligned to accelerate transformational change in specific neighborhoods. Focusing hiring practices on residents, more people will be able to own their home, walk to work and know their neighbors. Those results would help cut crime and give parents resources and time they need to support their children in school, which would improve academic outcomes and break the cycle of poverty family by family.

The Fourth Sphere and Scatter Diagram help to develop strategies that leverage tactics in all economic, infrastructure and human development spheres, empowering us to address all the critical causal factors while optimally using resources. Individuals have an opportunity to develop their strengths while the environment is changing around them. The challenge is to hold the vision for the whole while taking specific actions. As residents must be engaged in determining priorities and implementing strategies, finding people willing to provide neighborhood leadership is crucial. The same is true for a community as a whole. No one from the outside can provide effective help if community leaders are not willing or able to step up. Others cannot do for us what we must learn to do for ourselves. Problem solving is a local activity, both micro and macro. While outside technical support and resources are often needed, until a community becomes investment worthy, the approaches are often deficit based. Self-efficacy and transformation require positive individual and collective mindsets, a quality plan and behavioral changes. We build collective confidence by working together and producing results. Growth is a learn-by-doing exercise without a clear road map, requiring leaders who can thrive in ambiguity and are willing to risk failure.

Community Values

Answering "What is the problem?" is deeper than models and approaches. However, they can guide action and offer a framework for effective strategies for issues with cultural and deep historical roots. Some lessons from other communities and from other points in history can be extremely helpful.

One barrier we have encountered addressing poverty issues is the fierce and understandable anger of some people of color who believe whites are hypocrites and untrustworthy. They know poverty should never have happened and resulted from racism, oppression and exploitation. They can become enraged when they hear the voices of rigid ideology talk about self-made men, welfare queens and personal responsibility. This can lead to stalemate.

Others just want to focus on now and a path forward together, understanding that the founding ideals were a vision of what is possible. Rather than fret about how far we have to go to make visions real, I focus on the courage and strength of those who have moved us closer to the vision. Ironically, some of the most passionate warriors cannot stop fighting even when their perceived enemy is willing to lend a hand. Building a bridge to the future must become a shared undertaking if we are to get there at all.

What does a culture of stewardship look like? How do you create it? When we moved away from fragmented, committee-based efforts and began to focus on transformation, we knew we needed to do things differently. Shared values have proven to be a tool for learning a new approach and building vital trust. While we did not begin with a specific plan for their use, having a written set of values may well be one of the most important things we have done. By creating a shared mindset and operating system, we are building trust and learning new behaviors that have helped us collaborate across sectors, disciplines and interest groups.

To keep the values top of mind, a Fresno Business Council board member provides insights about a specific value at every meeting reminding everyone we must *be* the change, not just talk about it. Building a civic sector based upon shared values is an important element of transformational change. This requires a stewardship pipeline. High school student leaders attend our board meetings and report what they learned at a school board meeting and at their schools. We have learned much from them, too. The Human Element, a kindness initiative led by the student leaders of our largest school district, is a demonstration of their courage, understanding of the underlying problem and commitment to a better community.

The community values that have guided our work are:
- *Stewardship* – We will lead and follow as stewards of our region, caring responsibly for our community assets. We will work together to achieve the greatest, long-term benefit for the community as a whole.
- *Boundary Crossing and Collaboration* –We are willing to cross political, social ethnic and economic boundaries and partner with others to achieve community outcomes. We will lead "beyond the

walls" to create an inclusive, cohesive community through partnership and collaboration.

- **Commitment to Outcomes** – *We are willing* to take responsibility for tasks and achieving specified outcomes. We are committed to staying involved until the tasks are completed.

- **Art of the Possible Thinking** – We believe that anything is possible in the Fresno region. We will envision "success without limitations" and then backward map a specific, attainable strategy for achieving that vision.

- **Fact-Based Decision Making** – To the greatest extent possible, we will base decisions and action plans on objective data, thereby avoiding distortion of issues by personal feelings or agendas.

- **Truth Telling** – We value the empowerment of everyone involved, along with all community stakeholders, to honestly and forthrightly share all knowledge, experiences and insights relative to the work at hand. We take responsibility for ensuring our "truth" is current, not historical. We all share the responsibility for maintaining the truth telling standard.

- **Power Parity** – We respect all persons and recognize that there are diverse viewpoints. Positional power will not determine a strategy or preferred outcome, merit will. Viewpoints from diverse constituencies will be proactively sought to ensure the best possible outcomes for the community.

- **Commitment to Resolving Conflict** – Conflict is inevitable and is sometimes required in order to achieve the best outcomes possible. Healthy conflict involves valuing every individual regardless of his or her stance on a specific issue and an unwavering commitment to working through the conflict in a positive manner despite its severity.

- **Asset-Based Approach** – We are focused on using a strengths-based, asset-oriented approach to people and issues. We believe that positive change occurs when we appreciate, value and invest in what is best in our people and community.

- **Disclosure of Conflict of Interest** - We agree to disclose any personal or professional conflict of interest that may affect our objectivity before engaging in work that will impact the community. We seek to avoid even the appearance of impropriety.

To illustrate how applying our values gets results, Newby organized them by elements necessary for execution. .

I. Ethical Behavior = Trust
- *Stewardship*
- *Truth Telling*
- *Disclose Conflict of Interest*

II. Sound Business Practices = Effective Strategy & Accountability
- *Commitments to Outcomes*
- *Art of the Possible Thinking*
- *Fact-Based Decision Making*
- *Asset-Based Approach*

III. Best Teaming Principles = Results
- *Boundary Crossing & Collaboration*
- *Power Parity*
- *Commitment to Resolving Conflict*

The First Bus– The Strategic Team
We tried a variety of ways to grapple with critical issues, learning that no matter how many surveys or focus groups are done, regardless of socio-economic level, people basically identify the same goals. Fresno residents want safety; good jobs and prosperity; quality health care; great schools; beautiful, amenity rich neighborhoods; a thriving downtown; and a feeling of belonging. In a conceptual sense, these attributes could be expressed as the opportunity for all residents to enjoy life, liberty and the pursuit of happiness. It seems strange that even with nearly seven billion people on earth saying they want the same thing, we haven't been able to create it.

We have learned that central to our failure to create what we say we want is the lack of stewardship leadership and our collective willingness to follow. Many people who desire positions of power make promises, yet lack the strategic ability to deliver on them because they are unable to inspire trust and aligned action to achieve results. Oftentimes it is not until people are actually in office before they realize just how many constraints they have, how long it takes for significant success and how short their time of impact actually is. This helps explain why goals are often shallow enough to guarantee a ribbon cutting and press conference before leaving office and intractable issues are allowed to fester.

Working in Minnesota, I learned that to address substantive issues, you need more than advocates and good-government processes. You must have people who know how to solve problems – innovators and entrepreneurs, likely from the private sector – who can design and implement new systems or marshal constellations of existing assets. Early Fresno Business Council efforts to build teams by seeking volunteers yielded little. Those who have high-level strategic ability are unlikely to volunteer in an arena where they have little knowledge when they're successfully applying that expertise already. We also attempted the politically correct, more democratic method of identifying stakeholders and bringing all at the table, and ended up with a hodgepodge of people with different agendas, levels of ability and conflicts of interest. Most showed up for the first meetings, but came unprepared and were often unwilling to put in the time to deeply understand an issue much less commit to specific action. The ambiguity stage – where we must struggle with unknowns, resistance of the status quo and fear of failure – is when the most people drop out.

Finally, we would end up with a handful of stalwarts committed to finding a workable solution. Today, we simply start with the stalwarts. While I highly value notions of inclusion and a wide range of perceptions, there is a time when all that matters is talent and commitment. By thinking of everyone as a citizen first, not their day job or their area of passion, selection becomes as easy and the criteria are simple.

Once the community goal is clear, it's just about who has the talent to map a strategy and the skills to get it done. Mixing visionaries with strategic or tactical people at early stages can be a prescription for failure. It's about timing, respecting strengths and owning up to limitations. We call the model we adopted, based on these lessons, "The First Bus," patterned after what Jim Collins advised in *Good to Great—Why Some Companies Make the Leap....And Others Don't*. We work hard to identify the qualities needed in a team to understand an issue, discover the assets and efforts already in play to address it, and then craft an initial strategy. These teams are offline and time intensive.

The blue ribbon commission approach, with monthly meetings facilitated by an outside consultant, is the polar opposite, although in some cases it's needed to establish legitimacy and to tap into national best practices. Too often, though, it yields an expensive document that is added to many others sitting unread on desks for months before being laid to rest on a back shelf. Early on we tried this route and learned that it is not the highest and best approach for the Fresno Business Council.

The First Bus experience is fun and invigorating. Because there are no processes to follow and meetings are closed, candor, wit and conflict are mixed into a creative stew. Typically, the timeframe is limited, amping up the level of intensity and mutual commitment.

This approach is in stark contrast to those elected officials are forced to use largely due to the power broker, back room deals of the past. Limited by jurisdiction and formal authority, having to meet in public, targeted by increasingly mean-spirited media, and constantly being pressured by single interests, it's not surprising many elected bodies react or hide rather than solve problems. The rules limit development of collegiality, trust, innovation and collaboration. While some elected officials make terrific team members, most have developed other talents.

Strategic problem solvers and visionaries go where they are valued and rewarded. I have learned that most attempts to control bad behavior through regulations, rules and laws fail. Bad actors just do the next thing while everyone else pays the price in fees, time and frustration. Thus, the First Bus is aimed at positive solutions. While many of our examples focus on remediating poverty or other social issues, the approach can be applied to maximizing economic opportunities, too. In fact, it is by doing both at the same time that communities will have the best shot at transformational change. Working together across socioeconomic lines, citizens learn that simply giving money because they are moved by the plight of others is not a solution. Changing the economic game board is.

Innovation, Adaptability and Open-Mindedness
Our earlier efforts were largely advanced in a parallel universe. While elected officials and institutional leaders were involved, the focus was on actions and outcomes that could be accomplished without systemic changes within organizations. Learning how to collaborate across sectorial and organizational boundaries is an important step. However, it is unlikely to be enough to reach the "tipping point" necessary for cultural, sustainable and transformational changes. For that we need deeper and broader participation.

The current iteration of the Fresno Business Council includes a core team designed as a dynamic platform to take the lessons learned and insights from the past decade to scale. Most of us want the same outcomes, although we may differ in our beliefs about the best way to achieve them and who is responsible for which part. People who do not yet understand the reality of interdependence are often easily persuaded that there are direct causal relationships. They are unlikely to take the time to learn about the contextual underpinnings that lie beneath. In the stewardship space, individuals and organizations learn the importance of better understanding the breadth and complexity of intractable issues, their interdependence, and how to align decisions to maximize impact across systems and networks.

A concrete example is focusing on individual responsibility for health and expecting the "just do it" mantra to work. Change can be difficult for those with a job, health benefits, a car, access to quality grocery stores and a gym membership. It's is nearly impossible for someone who must cobble together multiple part-time jobs, depends upon public transportation, has no support network, and is under constant stress.

This is why Newby's scatter diagram, the Four Spheres and involvement of major institutions are so important if we are to successfully address intractable, chronic issues that have become systemic and endemic. Trying to solve such issues as poverty, crime, obesity and poor academic outcomes with singular focus is like putting a finger in a dike with many leaks and a big storm looming.

Government cannot solve these issues alone. Bigger bureaucracies with an eight-to-five workforce cannot build safe, inclusive, quality neighborhoods or a healthy, effective civic culture. That is the work of citizens – residents who take responsibility for themselves, their families, their neighborhoods and their communities. The term citizen is functional, not legal. Many legal residents aren't citizens; they just live here. Many undocumented residents gratefully embrace the responsibilities of citizenship. To solve intractable problems that result from a dysfunctional mindset and accompanying behaviors, citizenship must become epidemic, in its neutral meaning of widespread and endemic. It must sweep across the community and become self-perpetuating, something we pass along to others, particularly those in younger generations.

Intentional renewal and the transfer of knowledge and wisdom are essential elements of community vibrancy and sustainability which has less to do with form than substance. It is a state of mind where principles and lived experience speak more loudly than personalities or facts from another time. This requires humility from those eager to assume leadership positions and a willingness to let go and coach from those whose time has come to pass the torch.

The word "expert" must be held lightly. In a specific context, an expert may become clueless. In times of constant flux, the Zen concept of Beginner's Mind is a wise practice. Dean Kamen, a highly regarded inventor, gave us a memorable example of this principle when he challenged us to consider the original mission of a product or service before trying to repair or improve it. His illustration of this mindset led to a significant economic disruption, but liberated people chained to an oppressive health ritual. Rather than fix a pump that was malfunctioning on a hospital dialysis machine, he focused his firm's attention on the original mission of cleaning waste and fluid from a person's blood whose kidneys weren't working property. His team created a new apparatus that was compact, relatively inexpensive and could be used at home. The original mission was extending the quantity and quality of life for an individual suffering from kidney malfunction. The vehicle was simply a detail. His success sparked the creation of new businesses, made an old product obsolete, and resulted in hospitals losing a funding stream. Clearly, those in charge were stewards, not simply trying to maintain the status quo. The principle can apply to ideas and beliefs that no longer serve us.

Telos—*The End, Purpose or Goal of An Enterprise, Policy or Profession*
Telos – the intended purpose of an action – is a philosophical construct advanced by Aristotle and a central theme of this book. My sense is our lack of reflection and commitment to a philosophy of life has taken our culture off track. Founding principles and ideals must be renewed regularly to remain dynamic and widespread, but as Western culture sped up and materialism determined goals and what was measured, it was easy to forget our nation's original mission – liberty and justice for all.

Too many professionals are more concerned with winning than with justice. They teach what they know rather than what students need to learn. Their products cause harm or externalize costs to match profit projections. The price of losing *telos* crosses every dimension from personal angst and social collapse to environmental catastrophe and chronic poverty.

Unraveling the personal connections of community–what often happens when we put individual or single-interest goals ahead of long-term impact on the whole – is short-term thinking that can lead to decision-making without full consideration of consequences. Central to the culture of many indigenous peoples is considering the impact of decisions upon the next seven generations. We often fail to consider the impact on our own children much less tomorrow's – a sign that ambitious egos, not stewards, are in play.

Inspired by the thinking of Aristotle, Barry Schwartz and Kenneth Sharpe wrote *Practical Wisdom; Doing the Right Thing the Right Way,* which I devoured in two days after it was shared by a deeply reflective friend. We have all watched highly respected professionals devolve into commodities for sale, chasing dollars rather than solving problems and maintaining highest standards.

When I took the bar exam, I thought it odd that all of the questions were essay except the section on ethics, which was multiple choice. Of all the arenas where reflection is essential and ambiguity common, it is in applying the principles of ethics to real-life situations.

When a community or an entire country forgets its *telos,* a mean-spirited survival-of–the-fittest mentality can take hold and acts of desperation become commonplace. It can seem easier to go along in silence than to stand up for principles even if we're a university coach where a child molester is on the prowl; a broker in a firm where leaders are committing fraud; or a worker at a company making products that cause harm. While we must pick our battles, if we're honest with ourselves, we do know when it is our responsibility to act. We know when we fail to act, even if no one else knows. Damaged self-esteem may well be the greatest cost of all.

When did our country forget its *telos,* its mission to create liberty and justice for all? Do we still believe that everyone has intrinsic value and inalienable rights?

An honest, unflinching look makes clear our lack of commitment to these beliefs. Notions of fairness and equality can sound like naïve remnants of the past, not continuing responsibilities. Despite the warning that divided we would fall, fragmentation is all around us. Single interests have distorted politics at every level by ignoring responsibilities to the whole in favor of interest groups seeking special treatment and an inequitable amount of resources.

"America was established not to create wealth but to realize a vision, to realize an ideal - to discover and maintain liberty among men." Woodrow Wilson

The promise of capitalism has devolved in many minds into a belief that making money is the only bottom line. Powerful interests have become adept at protecting the status quo against the disruptions of entrepreneurs with better answers. As the web of the market and our retirement funds connects people of all stripes, we are all part of the system and blame is fruitless. The focus must be on what we should do now to restore values and how to rebuild a commitment from our public and private sectors to act with the best interests of the community in mind.

It begins with us.

We create the market and the private sector responds to it. If *we* are discerning and intentional about the quality and types of companies we support through our purchases, *we* can change the way the economy works.

We can elect representatives committed to ensuring that single interests do not distort the system.

We can create prosperity and a decent quality of life for everyone willing to do their part. Those with greater talents and a stronger work ethic will continue to earn more and achieve positions of greater influence. That is justice. Justice is also ensuring that everyone has quality opportunities and the supports needed to take advantage of them.

The issue is not who achieves the greatest success, but abuse of power. Those with greater gifts – call them the family heroes – can be seduced into believing that their role is more important and they should receive special treatment, completely forgetting those who sacrificed to make their success possible.

Capitalism is not an entitlement. It was secured through courage and service of those who rightly inspire gratitude and humility, whether they're parents, teachers or those buried at Arlington Cemetery. What matters is that we all remember that our freedom to pursue happiness was not easily won and could disappear if we are not vigilant in creating communities that offer opportunities for everyone.

Individuals who become disconnected from community are probably also disconnected from themselves. We are social creatures, dependent upon one another for material and spiritual sustenance. While becoming independent is an important rite of passage, the recognition of interdependence is the marker of maturity. Eventually, most realize accomplishments are shared endeavors. We are all standing on the shoulders of others and benefiting from their contributions.

What causes people to disconnect and communities to fragment? Trauma is at the root for many. People who experience abuse, discrimination or neglect when they're young can lose trust in humanity and life itself, believing the universe is a hostile place. Those born to privilege may cling to what they did not create by focusing on self rather than developing their innate talents. Ironically, some of the most entitled people can be those born to the greatest privilege.

In the '80s, we released the greed genie from the bottle. The decade's mantra seemed to be more is better and more makes me better. Whether it was accumulating wealth, positions or celebrity as an end in itself, many people succumbed to an addictive mindset at that time. The sterile emptiness of having it all and feeling empty inside is could be considered another form of poverty.

Many wealthy people wonder if they have friends or simply dependents and gold-diggers around them. A clue is whether or not they tell you the truth about your behavior.

This descent into materialism has played out in increasingly damaging ways in politics. Self-governance begins with personal mastery of and a commitment to self-actualization, not the acquisition of external power and position. Some therapists specialize in treating power addiction. While often coupled with other addictions such as sex or alcoholism, the need to be in charge, to be number one and to control other people can become an identity people defend at all costs.

Remember Lee Atwater, the good looking, political genius who master-minded the campaigns of Presidents Reagan and George H.W. Bush and engineered other Republican successes during the 1980s? Winning was the only thing that mattered. In a haunting article and a documentary before he died of brain cancer at 40, Mr. Atwater spoke eloquently to our challenge: "Long before I was struck with cancer, I felt something stirring in American society. It was a sense among the people of America – Republicans and Democrats alike – that something was missing from their lives – something crucial ... I wasn't exactly sure what it was. My illness helped me to see that what was missing in society is what was missing in me: a little heart, a lot of brotherhood." He went on to say, "What we need is a new politics of meaning. We need a new ethos of individual responsibility and caring. We need a new definition of civil society that fills us up again and make us feel like we are part of something bigger than ourselves."

As a philosophy major, recovering person and patriot, I took his message to heart. While I once had only venom for him, learning more filled me with compassion. Besides, I *was* him. At one time in my life, I wanted only to win, caring nothing about the implications for others. As I have never been involved in partisan politics and have long believed each party has pieces of the puzzle, I believe those who seek to divide us through fear and ideology are caught in the same trap Mr. Atwater and I were.

While some use the airwaves as a commodity not necessarily reflecting their beliefs, others are as self-righteous, narrow-minded and ignorant as they sound. Either way, considering what others sacrificed for freedom of the press and speech, it is disappointing how much *telos* has been lost from these vital cornerstones of American democracy.

As a champion of a more complete concept of capitalism and the opportunity for individual development of all citizens, I deeply valued moderates in both parties when I worked at Common Cause. They wanted to solve problems, not talk about them, and they had enough humility to realize that their answer was often incomplete. They did not lose their identity and become a politician, but remembered that they were first and foremost a citizen, leading as statesmen and stewards of the whole. Besides integrity and remembering the purpose of their position, these leaders also had another often-missing trait – wisdom. They made a causal connections, knowing that events and human behavior often aren't explicable in a linear way, which lifted them past the judgmental black–and–white thinking that marks today's politics. They took politics to a level of creative, transformational thinking essential to addressing complex challenges. No matter that this ability is innate or developmental, it offers a wormhole out of the stalemate created by linear polarization.

Two of the most useful types of interviews I conducted as a lobbyist were with electees before they assumed office and those who had announced their retirement. The excitement and enthusiasm of the newly elected are contagious. Campaign promises and the belief that one can make a difference shine like beacons in their minds and they can't wait to engage. The good government messages of Common Cause resonated with them. Doing the right thing for the right reason the right way was simply common sense. Sadly, as the pressures of single interests, personal ambition and party control increased, many lost their way.

Once they know they're leaving, the veneer of self-importance and need to defend against impossible demands or relentless media attacks start to melt. It's a time of personal reflection about what they had hoped to accomplish, what they succeeded in doing, how they grew as person, and where they compromised. In addition to valuable information about issues and people, retiring legislators often shared a sense of wistfulness and regret, pointing out when personal ambition became more important than making the decision they knew was right. When external identify becomes more important than inner knowing, we've given up more than we may realize.

The stress from living outside of our integrity can cause physical, emotional, mental and spiritual harm, and the symptoms may not present immediately or the lack of ease can become instantaneous. Thus, while living in accordance with our values and standing on principle may win accolades or get you killed, the deepest benefit is personal, keeping us healthy and at peace. It determines our quality of life.

As I was lobbying on behalf of the community as a whole, advocating for good-government issues and processes, I never had to "sell." I made it clear to all of the legislators that my goal was to simply ask them to do what they thought was right, not try to talk them into anything. Common Cause does not endorse candidates nor participate in fundraising. I avoided partisan events and was committed to working with everyone. When we organized a task force or commission, we were able engage activists who thought of each other as mortal enemies only to discover a soul mate. Their presumed foe simply saw a side of an issue that they could not see.

Sometimes the opportunity to work together on something of shared interest resulted in reconciliation or a solution to a separate issue that had become polarized. Once a relationship of trust is developed, the value is immeasurable. We must honor anyone who shows up because they care enough to engage.

81

To support people in doing the right thing, we tried a number of strategies in Minnesota. Clearly, the media play an important role by editorially praising those who demonstrate courage and challenging those who knuckle under to party or single-interest pressure. I worked closely with the capital reporters.

One of the most interesting approaches was convening an ethics retreat. Led by one of the private universities, we planned an overnight event in a natural setting where legislators, lobbyists and media representatives discussed ethics and politics.

Those who hang out at state capitals and endure session-end insanity know you develop a bond with those who share similar experiences whether you agree on issues or not. Add to that the Minnesota culture of candor and humility and we had the makings for fruitful conversations. While some discussion focused on rules and processes to provide a structure to support ethical decision making, the most important recommendations were personal – about the importance of mentorship, renewal and life balance. One thing we all agreed on – very rarely would anyone seek us out to tell us to do the "right thing." Most contact was about a single interest or self-interest. Finding sustainable, effective solutions amid the chaos of single interests has only become harder as complexity, speed and fragmentation increased. As Gardner said, "Everyone is organized except the people."

California is a great example in contrast. California state senators were invited to speak to our Senate's Ethics Committee about whether or not the Minnesota Legislature should go fulltime. The moment they left the hearing our senators were sold on *never* going there! While the Californians thought their approach was better, the Minnesotans recognized people who forgot they were citizens first, became attached to *being* an elected official and lost a sense of balance in their lives.

When we discussed this experience at the retreat, others confirmed we did not want to imitate California in going fulltime or in other aspects. Minnesota has steadfastly resisted the initiative process, too, with legislators believing it is their job to solve problems. Because it is a part-time legislature, they live with the consequences of their successes and failures and maintain citizen identities.

Also discouraging is how many rules and regulations are created in reaction to a handful of bad actors, a failure to pay attention, or an unpreventable event. Unnecessary controls and licenses end up costing businesses, employers and communities a fortune while the problems continue. Bad actors simply find another way, while those who want to do the right thing try to comply. How many occupations and service providers really need to be certified and regulated to protect the public? In the *Schumpeter Blog* of *The Economist*, a writer noted, "The cost of all this pettifoggery is huge – unless, that is, you are a member of one of the cartels that pushes for pettifogging rules or an employee of one of the bureaucratic bodies charged with enforcing them." Pettifoggery means quibbling over unimportant matters. Every rule and regulation has financial consequences. Those who have to change what they do or pay a fee have a cost, as do citizens who pick up the tab for enforcement. In aggregate, pettifoggery can add up to an unfriendly business environment, large government bureaucracies, and high tax rates.

Sadly, the biggest, often overlooked cost is chronic poverty. The barriers of complexity and fees that the poor face in starting businesses can be insurmountable. Resources that could be invested in empowerment strategies are siphoned off managing bureaucracies and compliance. For some, simply deciding to depend upon government programs or working off the grid is simply easier.

Many seem to experience life through the media whether films, television, talk radio, the Internet or newspapers and magazines. Indirect, digested experiences of others can prevent us from learning to think for ourselves and insulate us from taking responsibility for doing so. This can make it easy to ignore the hard work of difficult thinking and actual labor it takes to nurture a new idea into being.

It's particularly dangerous for youth prone to celebrate the wrong things or wanting quick fixes to soothe their existential, material or ego-based angst.

In the end, our culture will either support remembering *telos* or not. We can teach children to create and support a just and civil society at the same time we teach them marketable skills. We can be role models for the importance of lifelong learning and self-actualization rather than stop reading and learning as soon as we leave school. We can offer our children a vision quest and encourage them to think for themselves, or we can give them the answers and teach to the test.

Complexity and rapid change mean everyone will need to have real time problem-solving skills to thrive and survive. It is in our collective self-interest to create the conditions that empower everyone to develop his or her potential. *Telos* is at the core of an individual, organization or institution and remembering this through intentional renewal is our personal and shared responsibility.

Vertical Integration

Originating in mathematics, the concept of fractals has made its way into a number of disciplines. A fractal is a self-similar pattern that iterates without exactly replicating the original while maintaining key features. Fractal means broken, fractured or fragmented. These concepts set the stage for understanding the importance of vertical integration.

As we cede our collective power to higher levels of organization and government, the connection between what works, policies, and funding approaches often erodes. When top-down leaders forget the importance of hands-on experience, decisions can be ineffective if not outright destructive.

Add increasing fragmentation and self-serving attitudes and we end up with disembodied heads, not self-actualizing, authentic people in charge; easy targets for single-interest groups. In California, these interests have learned that the best bang for the buck is to focus on officials in Sacramento and not worry about communities.

The Ralph M. Brown Act's open-meeting rules while important for transparency can also make building a team challenging and inhibit California lawmakers from trying to solve problems or address complex, controversial, and difficult issues. In other words, there are structural barriers to problem solving that changing legislators won't or can't fix.

At Common Cause, I initially believed good government was enough. If we just got the process right, the answers would emerge and we could solve any problem. But I came to realize people who don't know one another can become little more than a concept or even an object. We need visionaries to think outside of time and space; strategists to align seemingly random assets into constellations that leverage resources; and action and results-driven tactical doers to keep their hands on the wheel and their eyes on their to-do list. It may sound trite, but diversity is our greatest strength rings true. Yet, the concept has too often been narrowed to race although the most important diversity in problem solving has more to do with life experiences, temperaments, mental models and various intelligences.

Each community has different assets, challenges, leadership and capacity, so trying to solve its problems through state or federal government has proven to be both illusive and expensive. One size does *not* fit all. Having shared standards makes sense, but if you don't consider dissimilar starting points, a standard can become punitive rather than inspiring. Those born on third base often have no understanding of the challenges of those born in the dugout, yet they tend to have more influence on remedies and measurements. In a more-is-better, survival-of-the-fittest mentality, this approach can make sense: Make the grade or don't. In community, this approach can sound ridiculous. When many people live in gated communities and many more are locked behind bars on the taxpayer's dime, we clearly haven't thought deeply about human development.

It's both dumb and expensive to react to destructive and desperate behavior with punishment and rejection rather than taking time to deeply understand the problems and fashion solutions that change underlying conditions. Smart solutions save money and develop people. We become committed to smart solutions when we remember our founding principles, remember to be grateful and remember it's not all about us.

We created higher levels of government for the same reason we created government. Some things we cannot do alone. We must pool resources and talents. Basic infrastructure is a shared asset and responsibility. We need roads, transportation, water pipes and sewers. We aggregate our resources to create amenities like parks, stadiums and cultural venues. We pool our money to educate all our children without limits imposed by circumstances of birth. Unfortunately, although it's in our self-interest to help, we have allowed some schools to be subpar, lacking resources and talents to help the children with developmental gaps, exacerbated by parents lacking the knowledge, time or money to ensure their children can succeed.

Our levels of government are also interdependent and significant dysfunction at any level affects them all. As more power and money default upwards, approaches lack the customization necessary to be effective. Single interest influences distort them even more. When it's our community and our children paying the price for misguided public policy, we are more likely to do something about it. Yet, many citizens have chosen to be spectators and consumers. Rather than being a result of apathy or cynicism, many people give up because they feel overwhelmed when the challenge becomes bigger than taking on city hall and they don't know how to seek redress at a higher level of government.

Incrementally, we have created a monster of over-regulation and underperformance, throwing billions of hard-earned dollars against a mighty fan that sends dwindling amounts back in disconnected drops. No wonder so many communities are drying up and not bearing the fruits of prosperity. Extremely large and diverse states like California experience even tougher challenges because of unique regional assets and challenges and different levels of civic capacity. Because of the political focus on Sacramento, citizens haven't banded together sufficiently to create what is important in each region.

Instead, regions have competed against one another for the state's largess. Playing survival-of–the-fittest typically means the richest and most-influential ensure concentrated areas of great wealth and environmental beauty, while other areas languish. Poor regions have been treated more like plantations or resource colonies rather than worthy of equal, if not remedial treatment.

Lack of parity is an easy choice when those who can win at the expense of others choose to focus on narrow, self-interests rather than the common good. While in the short term this approach does achieve results, a long-term perspective exposes how foolhardy it is. Every region is part of the same state ecosystem. As a nation, we share the planet with other nations making up an interdependent natural and economic ecosystem that seems to be getting smaller by the day. Whether it's the global economy, air and water conditions, or issues of poverty and health, no issue is just local anymore.

We either find a way to align and leverage resources or the complex, intractable issues of our time will remain so and we will go down together as a species. An environmentalist told me he laughs when people tell him they're worried about the earth surviving. He tells them the earth will be fine. The issue is whether or not humanity will be on it. When I shared this with a colleague, he laughed and said there are scientists who think the earth will turn into Venus if we don't wise up.

Achieving vertical integration requires both bottom-up and top-down application. Taking the fractal notion and considering core values, size is not the issue. Like Russian nesting dolls that repeat a pattern but are all unique, we can replicate the mindset and operating system of the Four Spheres and Community Values at every disc along the backbone.

Whether an issue is local, regional, state, national or global, a holistic mindset and commitment to operating in accordance with shared values can be applied. While difficult initially, because stewardship is counter-cultural and can lead to economic disruption, it does get easier as more people recognize its merit in terms of hard dollars, moral decency, and common sense. We also need more people to master the art of peacemaking alongside policymaking. The more successful we are; the more others will join in the movement.

Bottom-up is about values, customized strategies, citizen engagement and measuring results that matter. Top-down is about ensuring that policies and resources at all levels align behind local strategies and are effective. Top-down is also about standards and investing additional resources in communities that are willing, but aren't quite ready.

Building a sturdy civic infrastructure takes time, trust and practice. We can share lessons learned, but we must apply them ourselves. Investing public dollars in communities neither willing nor ready is no different from enabling an addict unwilling to change. Out of compassion, too many of our policies have enabled, rather than empowered people.

It takes an authentic relationship to discern the core issues and hold someone accountable. Wounded people without self-awareness, whether the family hero or the scapegoat, are often angry and feel like victims. With hearts and minds closed, it is unlikely that they will formulate, fund or help execute a transformational solution. Readiness as a pre-requisite for assistance can spark the motivation for change that simply treating needs can extinguish.

Communications

"What we have here is a failure to communicate." No kidding!

Boomers and movie buffs no doubt remember this clarifying statement from the Paul Newman film *Cool Hand Luke*. However, Luke understood and refused to comply, just as more and more people are no longer are willing to comply when a principle is involved. Whistle blowers, advocates and citizens of all stripes are standing up to hypocrisy and the failure of outdated ideas and systems. We've lost faith in institutions that no longer serve us and are the product of our educational focus on memorization and accepting beliefs of those in authority rather than teaching children critical thinking.

Today, we need dynamic partnerships where people at all levels of an enterprise are encouraged to share what they see and know so informed decisions can be made throughout. Shifting to a dynamic culture is not easy, but doing nothing and allowing organizations, families and communities to collapse is not an option. The American DNA is a blend of courage and innovation and we see signs of awakening spirit in communities everywhere.

Our communications strategy is multifaceted because important audiences are so different. As we gain momentum and move beyond the pioneers, there are many developmental stages to remember. It took nearly two decades of concentrated intellectual and hands-on effort to develop a framework to deeply understand issues and assets. It takes time to build platforms and relationships needed to advance comprehensive strategies and overcome siloed thinking and action. As more results become visible and measurable, we are confident those who don't trust a new approach until it's demonstrated will join us on a new path.

Most people learn best through experience. If others don't believe you or can't replicate it, a solution won't happen or hold. Massive citizen engagement and sticky solutions to intractable problems are indivisible. It may take longer and try everyone's patience, yet when we finally arrive we not only achieve a solution, we develop greater capacity and a shift in culture.

An A on the test when all you did was memorize answers is pseudo learning. This doesn't prepare us for life. Learning through trial by error not only solves problems but cultivates problem-solving skills for other challenges and develops confidence to lead.

One of our most creative board member's, Mike Wilhelm, created a two sided jigsaw puzzle as a teaching tool. One side has the Four Spheres, the other our scatter diagram. This simple tool communicates a framework to think, organize and act. As a metaphor for community, a jigsaw puzzle additionally offers a number of key messages. Who doesn't keep the box top handy to refer back to what the final product is supposed to look like?

Most of us turn all the pieces over so we know where they fit before forging ahead –frame first, then specific areas such as sky, water, trees, people or whatever suits our fancy. Jigsaw puzzles are family and friends projects, a vehicle to socialize and work together toward a common goal, illustrating how a community fits together. There are deeper messages when thinking about a jigsaw puzzle as a community. There are no extra pieces. All the pieces may be the same size, but each is unique and has a specific role. The puzzle isn't complete until every piece is in place. Building a prosperous, healthy and whole community follows the same process when self-governance and liberty and justice for all are guiding principles for the vision on the box.

Because the framework is where we begin, the first target for communication has been thought leaders – the community's positional and influential people. What they believe to be reality can lead to the game board upon which we all play. They make up the rules and determine the winners.

Because the economic sphere tends to be the most powerful and the most generative, beliefs and ideas from this arena often spill into the other spheres in obvious and subtle ways. Thus, it is vitally important that business schools, professional schools and industry associations are part of ongoing communication networks focused on the civic sector.

A challenge in communicating with the private sector is that it is not a monolith. If you say "business" around traditional chamber of commerce members, they think brethren. Say "regulation," "fees" or "licensing" and many simply see red; against them on principle. The concept of a healthy business climate typically isn't customized in their minds.

At Common Cause and the Fresno Business Council, I have learned a lot about different sizes of business and their needs: from a solo practitioner or entrepreneur to large operations that compete nationally and internationally. The level of sophistication across this broad range of enterprises requires careful communication to achieve desired impact.

To ensure the message of transformation isn't lost, I approach business people first as citizens, recognizing that many in this sector care passionately about a broad range of issues. Approaching them as just their day job first is ineffective and even disrespectful.

But for a few constant travelers, everyone lives somewhere and is multidimensional. Our community enriches our lives whether we attend to its needs or not. Thinking of everyone as a citizen first levels the civic playing field by acknowledging our shared interests.

By engaging extraordinarily talented business people as citizens and preparing them to lead from the Fourth Sphere, we can attract the talent essential to tackling massive, systemic issues and keep them engaged, making them increasingly valuable. Long-term engagement also helps to shift their focus from a short-term business climate analysis to how actions will affect the community and our shared future.

What is in the best interests of the community usually is in the best interests of desirable businesses that add value and compete on merit. However, this is not the case for companies that focus exclusively on profit and are allowed to externalize costs to the environment, their workers or the community.

It's also not the case for those industries that target human weakness and the most vulnerable among us such as pornography; violence in films, television, music and games; gambling; and junk food. Powerful industries like gas and oil, insurance and pharmaceuticals, have enough influence to stop better solutions as the tobacco industry did with nonsmoking sections on airplanes. Compromise without values at the core can mean building half a bridge.

Truth often leads to both economic disruption and opportunity. As Winston Churchill said, "The truth is incontrovertible. Malice may attack it, ignorance may divide it, but in the end, there it is."

Unfortunately, many of those who are anti-business think in terms of its shadow players, not the hard-working community-minded people that are by far the sector's majority. I believe the fastest path to a healthy, business-friendly environment is to increase business steward engagement in work of the community. With their expertise, strategic sense and organizational skills they can align the regulatory environment to support value-adding goods and services while holding accountable companies that do harm or externalize costs.

It's easy to say consumers and the market will take care of bad actors, but most consumers are uninformed, while bad actors simply organize, bundle money and influence policy. Those trying to do the right thing are left with even more barriers to growth and productivity. Legislating to control those without conscience has led to an incomprehensible tax code and volumes of confusing, maladaptive regulations for all industries and sectors. Said a colleague, "California micromanages every sector resulting in paralysis and exodus!"

Many audiences must be reached to achieve transformation. While understanding the concepts, our shared history, execution and citizenship are important, reaching the heart is essential. Remembering why, having hope and a sense of purpose, and feeling a connection to something greater than oneself are pathways to kindling passion, the source of motivation. Without a passion for learning, it's easy to hang onto beliefs and "facts" that have become outdated and deemed flatly wrong. It may seem like the end of the road, but looking deeper we may have simply found an opening into the next great mystery.

We've learned we must figure out how to connect to people where they are with people they already know and trust. One by one, customized communication, while seemingly inefficient, is sustainable, scalable and a long-term investment. Change from the inside out, where both the heart and mind engage, is building on rock not quick-fix quicksand. When the culture is the problem, people choosing to align one by one are the solution. An inspiring vision is a giant magnet pulling the individual metal filings to True North. Slow, yes, but how has fast been working for us?

> *"Electric communication will never be a substitute for the face of someone who with their soul encourages another person to be brave and true."* Charles Dickens

As a final point on communication and its relationship to community building, Rollo May said, "Communication leads to community, that is, to understanding, intimacy and mutual valuing." The Latin root of communication is *munus* and has to do with gifts or duties offered publicly. At a workshop based upon their book *Abundant Community – Awakening the Power of Families and Neighborhoods,* John McKnight and

Peter Block brought our jigsaw puzzle to life with examples of resources already available if we got to know one another. We learned we are enough and we have enough if we worked together.

One of the high points at Common Cause was chauffeuring Archibald Cox, the national board chairman, when he traveled to Minnesota. As a pivotal player in Watergate, his perspective of that time taught me about the perils of Washington politics and the heroic efforts many have made to preserve our founding ideals.

Discussing the challenge of solving complex problems, he told me something that has guided my work: "When you have community, you can solve any problem. When you don't, you won't but you will spend a whole lot of time and money trying." If we believe our fates are not intertwined and we compete for scarce resources, we will create a world of scarcity and cutthroat competition. If we remember that life is a paradox – we are both separate and one – we can work together to create abundance.

Steward Leadership—Execution

Understand the problem? Check. Crafted a comprehensive strategy. Check. Clarified outcomes? Check. Pulled together a community coalition. Check. What is missing? The private sector knows the most important element is leadership. Venture capitalists want to know who is on the leadership team and about their track record. A great idea does not an outcome make. Without an effective CEO function, a great idea and plenty of resources remains inert.

In the public and nonprofit sectors, leadership is often considered overhead. Rather than recognize it is a critical success factor, boards are often made up of people who could never lead an organization or earn a top salary. They quibble over salary sometimes because of political considerations or even jealousy. Somehow communities think the best of the brightest should work hard to develop their talents, acquire knowledge and test their mettle but sacrifice the quality of life their family would enjoy in the private sector and come to work at a low salary. For some, this works. Yet, clearly not enough are willing to do this. Despite the fact that our communities are at stake and failure impacts us all, we have been largely unwilling to reward those with the level of talent needed to succeed. You get what you pay for. Rather than trust in their leadership, another barrier is the byzantine processes expected of them to move an agenda forward. Quite often the best leaders must be recruited and their condition, active engagement and support.

In one of Mohammed Yunis' books he gave an example at Dannon. Rather than charitable gifts, the company had a charitable arm that solved community problems. Those working for the company had a choice. For the same salary they could work on either side of the business. As younger generations are seeking to serve their communities, imagine the impact of this approach across a broad range of companies.

While we have had outstanding volunteers step up and serve as steward leaders, a sustained focus and mastery of new skills takes time. Major initiatives are lifestyle jobs. In most cases, we believe they will attract people mid-career, those who have already been successful. The attributes of these leaders are: impartial, no ideology, high integrity, strategic thinker, conflict manager, risk taker and accountable. This is a potent package. Their value is immeasurable. They bring out the best in everyone. They transform intractable issues into solvable ones.

Chapter 14

FROM THE TITANIC TO

THE ENTERPRISE

Achieving and sustaining a higher level of thinking is difficult. By combining the frameworks and key concepts in earlier chapters with a commitment to acting in accordance with community values, a new path seems to magically appear. We call it the Fourth Sphere. Some call it the fourth dimension or fourth sector.

In practical terms, it means beginning again with the mission in mind unlimited by existing thought or physical forms. Gardner called it renewal. Zen practitioners call it Beginner's Mind. It adds up to humility and courage; a realization that you don't know, no one else does, and that we must explore the unknown.

Typically only a handful of scouts will lead into the abyss, but that's all you need. A preliminary step is accepting that we have reached a dead end and exhausted all known possibilities. As the innovators and pioneers set out, some will believe that if we just work harder, faster and longer we can fix any problem. Sometimes they're right.

It's possible, however, they're simply tidying up the Titanic. Entrepreneurs learn to fail fast and try the next thing. Failure is a learning opportunity, not a judgment and the quest can be exhilarating. The reasons for exploring a reset can vary. Sometimes, the challenge has become too complex. At some point, none of the disciplines has enough knowledge, wisdom or resources to meet the need no matter the effort. In other cases, a discovery is the catalyst.

It is amazing how many facts are falling like dominoes as science pursues understanding of the great mystery as mystics keep moving the goal posts. As an attorney I learned we made it all up and if the rules weren't resulting in a just or intended outcome, we should change them. Had we not merged the court of law with the court of equity in our country, we could still step outside of precedent and do what a judge, assumed to be wise, believes is right.

Instead of this adaptive, reality-based path, our culture locked down judges in some areas and a host of others into a one-size-fits-all compliance approach, which rewards doing things right at the expense of doing the right thing. Vestiges of the Industrial Age are all around us in our thinking, systems and organizational structures. The material yield from this approach has been spectacular and has improved the quality of life for many people. However, as the economic engine grew bigger, like a runaway train sustainability has become a major issue.

Some companies have maintained a level of balance and many are adapting to sustainable practices, but the economic disruption inherent in a triple bottom line (think profit, people, and planet) approach is significant. Working together to manage the transition is the most pragmatic path. While too slow for some and too fast for others, trying to force changes or stop activities via law suits and vilification bring us to stalemate.

When most believe in the same game, why fault the winners? Many simply accept what is and declare they are just being realistic, dismissing visionaries as dreamers, naïve to the way the world works. Yet, if we made it all up and the dream has turned into a nightmare, it's time to make up a new game. We need dreamers, architects and those who execute working together, not pointing fingers at one another.

97

Large, global companies with roots nowhere are disembodied. Like a person lacking emotional or physical feeling, they are capable of cruelty and exploitation. While people numb feelings through addictions, corporations never had them in the first place. The importance of values-based regulation and accountability grows the larger the edifice.

It bears repeating, capitalism is not an entitlement, but earned through the sacrifices of freedom fighters. When business leaders, boards and stockholders forget they're citizens first, responsible to the past and the future, they are more likely to make short-term decisions that dishonor our forebears and jeopardize our children's future. Quarterly reports, like relentless student testing, have undermined the mission of both business and education.

Because the economic sphere plays such an important role in a community's quality of life, I will attempt to apply the frameworks to this arena first. As the Four Spheres are interdependent, I will include the implications on the other spheres.

Before I worked for the Fresno Business Council, I had a limited understanding of how the economy worked and where the levers of change resided. From afar, it looks like the private sector is free standing. However, a closer look reveals that many private firms do a lot of business with government, education and nonprofits. Whether products are used by the military, textbooks for education, software applications, or food for cafeterias, the degree to which the private sector depends upon taxpayer dollars is significant.

This raises the issue of who gets things done better and cheaper and when you're the customer, producer or taxpayer. As Upton Sinclair said, "It is difficult to get a man to understand something when his salary depends upon his not understanding it." This underscores how important it is that we think of ourselves first as citizens and stewards of the whole, collectively responsible for policy making. Impartiality is the parent of a healthy and prosperous community.

I reviewed a range of opinions about the purpose of the economy. My conclusion: It is to produce goods and services to improve the quality of life in communities; provide employment and entrepreneurial opportunities; generate wealth for individuals; and produce resources for government to create shared infrastructure, amenities and public services.

As a young person, I was inspired by Ayn Rand's escape from communism and her passion for freedom. I suspect her philosophy resonates soundly with the family heroes. Today, I believe we must embrace a more comprehensive concept of capitalism. There are many paths to achieving self-reliance. We need to develop policies and infrastructures that support a smorgasbord of choices to match the innate abilities of individuals and the needs and desires of specific communities. Our failure to do this will continue to exclude people from the community and their prospects for self-reliance. The costs for social programs and a justice system to address their deficits will remain the giant sea anchor stopping communities from prospering.

The fractal concept comes into play here. If all businesses are designed with community values at the core, size is not the issue, although the larger an entity becomes the tougher it may be to sustain them. In large companies, departments and unions often fight over the budget. Without a CEO who focuses only on the desired outcomes, intramural sports can take down the entire enterprise. And the same holds true for a political jurisdiction – local, state or national.

We need people working at every level of the economy and enterprises to align decisions with shared values aimed at shared outcomes. Improving the quality of life for all is a shared responsibility whether you're a hospice worker or lead a major manufacturer exporting around the world. The rights of citizenship bestow the opportunity to pursue our happiness, but its responsibilities require us to ensure that everyone has opportunity.

The alternative is thousands out of work, ill-prepared for the workplace, defeated and despairing, creating a morass of social problems that no amount of working harder by those succeeding or marginally subsisting in the game will ever overcome. We must turn and face our shadow if we are to become whole and create sustainable prosperity. We need to exchange the Monopoly game board for one that will result in a different picture leading to manifesting the American Dream.

Chapter 15

NOT BY BREAD ALONE—WHAT HAPPENED TO THE FOOD SUPPLY?

Food is a hot topic, affecting us in such fundamental ways that exploring how we ended up with so many obese, malnourished people is a worthy undertaking.

Numerous documentaries have detailed our journey from eating whole, locally grown foods that support a wide range of jobs to where we are today. Homemade and shared were common traditions in neighborhoods when potlucks and backyard barbecues were the mainstay of many people's social lives.

Our accelerated more-and bigger-is-better culture swept through the food industry like a wildfire, shrinking local distribution models and infrastructure and causing people to think food comes from a grocery store not a farm. In allowing the severance of ties to the agricultural community and our land, we lost a vital part of our history and connection to the natural world. Convenience, low cost, and saving time were key drivers from the consumer side. As women joined the work force, home cooked devolved into packaged and frozen as the family dinner table hosted drive by meals.

In the 1950s, a stop at the few fast-food places was a rare event. Today fast food is the cornerstone of many people's diets, most tragically children. Food deserts, where there are no grocery stores, and food swamps, places laced with fast food outlets, tend to overlap in poorer communities, adding to our nation's obesity epidemic. Add parents working multiple jobs, kids left alone and dangerous streets, it's no surprise that children in these neighborhoods do poorly in school and their health can be permanently damaged.

Neuroscience and other fields have come a long way in explaining "you are what you eat." Without adequate nourishment, the brain performs poorly, leading to the inability to concentrate and a lack of energy. Poor nutrition is also implicated in the development of and failure to heal from a range of mental illnesses. Research suggests that traumas can also damage brain function, which can lead to cravings and intense emotions that can result in addictions and violence.

Looking only at behavior is an inadequate way to assess the situation, much less determine effective solutions. Food is a central component of a transformation strategy, offering a path to restoring neighborhood-level economies while improving health, education and public safety outcomes.

Ironically, Fresno sits in the middle of one of the world's most productive agricultural regions, yet it hosts some of the worst obesity and diabetes in the nation. Much of the food we grow is earmarked for processers and markets outside the area, so we have an opportunity is to build a vibrant local and regional food system alongside the large players who grow, pack, process and export food. Getting the food back highly processed through fast food outlets and the middle aisles of grocery stores is not a good bargain for our area.

Tapping existing assets and filling gaps in distribution is a path to building a system that uses food to improve the quality of life of residents, create wealth, generate resources for government services and build community. From the Fourth Sphere, food is a treasure trove that can affect every sphere in positive ways if we are intentional and utilize values based upon it. While a national movement to restore regional food systems will look different in every community, a holistic and values-based approach would fit well with our agenda. Playing off of successful cooperative business models, food offers a way to complete the concept of capitalism with co-ops, social businesses and sheltered workshops.

One of the most complete strategies for achieving a triple bottom line regional food system is Food Commons. People around the country who are passionate about quality food and equitable economies and collectively have vast experience in food systems, operational models, finance, law and health produced the concept paper. Local prototypes are moving forward in Fresno, Atlanta and New Zealand. One of the goals is to make the value chain transparent and ensure equitable remuneration for farmers, who take the greatest risk, while ensuring fair wages to farmworkers and food service employees.

Laws address issues of minimum wage and working conditions, but in some industries they have been inadequate, sustaining a long history of "invisible" workers living at the margins of society. Undocumented or exploited workers may be concentrated in some regions, but they and their children attend our schools, require medical attention and get involved in the justice system. Pay now or pay later is reality, and later is often more expensive.

New business models can enhance different levels of the economy and produce a range of jobs, however, it is not enough to address the economic aspects of food. As noted in the HBO, Kaiser Permanente supported documentary *The Weight of the Nation*, we live in a hostile food environment, where cheap food is available nearly everywhere 24/7. Marketing experts tantalize with consumer-seducing commercials. Portion size based upon the bigger-is-better craze has taken hold of producers and consumers. The consequences are multidimensional, severe and costly. Some products aren't really food at all, lacking vital nutrients, but adding harmful chemicals to human bodies already bombarded with chemicals in the air, water and soil. And the most vulnerable – our poor, the traumatized and children – are most likely to consume excess amounts of these products, sending them on a downward spiral as health and opportunities deteriorate.

Given the number of food programs to address hunger and the smorgasbord of related activities by the U.S. / Department of Agriculture and state agencies, it is hard to explain the poor quality of food in our nation. Where does the notion of *telos* fit? There are other questions, too. If one purpose of the economy is to improve quality of life, how much of the food on grocery store shelves and bins will actually do that? How many businesses are involved in marketing, packaging, processing and distributing food and beverages implicated in obesity and other health issues?

Virgil, the Roman poet, said, "The greatest wealth is health." Despite our advanced health-care system, Americans might be considered poor by Virgil's measure. While it's easy to rant about fake food, misinformation and toxic chemicals, a physician friend reminds me that the chemists and other scientists who came up with this stuff thought they were doing a good thing. Where once artificial sweeteners, flavors and fats sounded healthy; today most health-conscious people avoid them.

Knowledge causes economic disruptions. As more consumers demand and purchase whole and organic foods more businesses get into these markets. At the same time, those wedded to old business models and products have more political clout. The status quo always does, leaving it up to policymakers and consumers, acting as citizens first, to ensure our system delivers healthy, affordable food to everyone.

The costs of not doing so, in terms of health care, lower productivity, mental health and the justice system are staggering compared to creating the infrastructure and other supports necessary to accomplish this. Some may not remember we used to subsidize tobacco and companies marketed their products as healthy stress relievers. Ironically, smokers knew the first time they lit up that cigarettes are bad for us. The body's reaction, if it could speak, would have to be bleeped. But the collective time between knowing and doing was decades.

Vertical alignment would look like policies across many agencies and systems focused on increasing awareness and enhancing local food systems that distribute healthy, whole food. The Farm Bill and many federal programs can support specialty crops and build their market share. Zoning and licensing can be aligned to create neighborhood-level access in communities where fresh fruits and vegetables have been unavailable or overpriced. Schools and other institutions have a huge role to play in purchasing, education and support.

Making health a priority in all policies requires being informed and intentional. Every health educator and provider has a role to play along with every employer. However, widely enjoyed health and well-being and a culture supporting wellness would create a massive economic disruption. Most healthcare providers are not closed systems like Kaiser Permanente, where keeping members healthy is in their economic self-interest. Most players in the industry and the systems that process claims, provide drugs and perform surgery gain economically if you are sick and have adequate insurance or the government is paying. One of the most common reasons for individual bankruptcy is being overwhelmed by healthcare costs.

Efforts to reform our national healthcare system have been a presidential quest since the 1900s. Enactment of the Patient Protection and Affordable Care Act in 2010 promised broad reforms and healthcare for millions previously without coverage. Its implementation in 2013, however, was rough for potential beneficiaries, healthcare providers and government agencies. A political firestorm ignited, indicating the long national healthcare debate wasn't fully resolved.

I remember debating with the speaker of the Minnesota House of Representatives about health care. We both wanted a healthy population and resources for those who suffered medical misfortune, but disagreed about strategy. His goal was to pass legislation to guarantee universal healthcare, while I believed we had to also aggressively address prevention through education and other means stressing personal responsibility and accountability. It was the difference between state and community-level perspectives. Universal health care without universal responsibility for self-care, I believed, would be the worst kind of enabling, with huge costs unfairly distributed to others. As we argued, the speaker puffed on a cigarette standing on the floor of the House of Representatives even though smoking had been banned in public buildings for years. He was demonstrating my point and I didn't hesitate to point it out.

In politics the rhetoric often mixes up responsibility and accountability. Responsibility means the ability to respond, as opposed to react. When an individual has the awareness, tools and resources to make a choice, healthy or not, holding them accountable financially and in other ways makes sense. When they're not able to choose, accountability and blame could be considered a form of bullying and ignorance.

People born to privilege and the middle class often fail to understand that what they learned automatically, their fellow citizens born to poverty may not know. After reading books by Ruby Payne and *Pedagogy of the Oppressed* by Paolo Freire, I retired my belief that if people just worked harder they could make it.

A successful manufacturer in Michigan who hires people off welfare shows his staff the documentary *A Day in the Life of Poverty* to help them understand. When we take the time to understand and meet people where they are, we can work together to design more effective approaches recognizing that everyone has their own story. One-size-fits-all and mindless subsidies based purely upon need are bound to be ineffective whether we're addressing health or financial challenges.

Another challenge we face in creating a support system leading to widespread health is that Western medicine is largely reactive.

Changes in understanding the importance of aligning body, mind and spirit have given birth to countless new methodologies and the revival of the older, more-natural approaches of the wisdom traditions. Many of those with resources have already adopted healthy lifestyles that include active stress management through meditation and exercise, herbal remedies and body work including chiropractic, massage and reflexology. While Western medicine is a welcome backup whose role in certain specialties and emergencies is essential, the most-educated health consumers today take responsibility for their own health.

Popping a pill to treat symptoms rather than losing weight is both irresponsible and self-destructive. Others pick up part of the tab and the individual shoulders the consequences of ill-health. Changing health habits is difficult and requires serious motivation and support, but it's clear a sickness-treatment approach is insufficient. Health insurance is an oxymoron. It does not ensure health, it insures partial payment if the cost falls within specific guidelines.

If we were to begin again, how would we design an American approach to health promotion and care? Who would be engaged? Who would be held accountable for what? Sometimes an iterative approach of incremental improvements is appropriate, but when institutions have lost their *telos* and science has catapulted us to new understandings, whole-scale transformation is the best path. Because we have terrible health statistics, too few professionals, a lack of essential infrastructure and a very diverse population with large pockets of concentrated poverty, simply chasing the old system with more dollars is unlikely to have the impact we seek.

Applying the Four Spheres, our Scatter Diagram, community values, *telos*, vertical and horizontal integration, coalition of the willing, regional customization and tapping best practice innovations, we could design a system tailored to our unique needs building upon our existing assets. Rather than begin top down, we could begin bottom up, making prevention and personal responsibility the central focus.

We could design neighborhoods or restore them to ensure walkability, recreational opportunities, safety and access to healthy food. We could create a distributed model of intervention where minor health issues and prevention protocols could be administered in neighborhood clinics within schools, churches or vehicles.

Using precision medicine – 50 basic health issues have defined treatment approaches – lower-level health practitioners could provide triage with a system of referrals should greater expertise be necessary. Telemedicine offers diagnosis and treatment options that can bring specialists to individuals, rather than incurring the costs of travel. Inventor Thomas Edison predicted where healthcare was headed when he said, "The doctor of the future will give no medicine; but will interest his patients in the care of the human frame, in diet, and the cause and prevention of disease."

Working across institutions, employers can change the culture, helping recast living a healthy lifestyle as a responsibility of citizenship balancing the right to healthcare. In an ecosystem, what one does affects the whole. In a community, we have both individual and collective responsibility. If more of us practiced self-care, there would be plenty of resources for those who suffer from genetic and random health challenges or have an unfortunate accident. Allowing people to fall into bankruptcy due to health care costs affects every creditor and our economy as a whole. We are all part of the problem and the solution.

A transition to a new culture of health and a new system to support it may be a slow process, but it's well underway. The health-literate already have changed behaviors, becoming advocates for policy and system changes. Divided efforts to advance pieces of the puzzle are uniting and achieving greater impact.

A broad continuum of people focused on remediating poverty are exploring economic solutions rather than depending upon government. Rigid institutional representatives of teachers unions, chambers of commerce, industry and religious organizations are losing ground within their own groups. Meanwhile former political party members "decline to state," acknowledging that extremists and single interests "don't speak for me."

When enough people realize that winning is losing if their gain harms the community, the power of single interests and corruption will continue to diminish. The great thing about a value-based, Four Sphere approach is transferability to other issues. Potential allies are everywhere. An awakening to a hunger for purpose and significance is growing stronger in America.

I suspect the final chapter of the boomers will be the transformation of institutions and a revitalization of the American Spirit and Dream. For example, the majority of boomers are likely to embrace the hospice movement and gracefully live until they die rather than attempt to linger through extraordinary measures. (It is estimated more than 60 percent of an individual's healthcare costs often are incurred during the last six months of life.)

Those who protested against hypocrisy in their youth are poised to become stewards, building the next version of America and a pipeline of emerging stewards to build upon scaffolding rather than relearn the lessons of community after hitting bottom yet again.

Chapter 16

AS A MAN THINKETH

Applying the framework and principles to the challenge of mental health has wide-ranging implications. Mental health and its absence are as ubiquitous as air, energy and water.

I look at mental health as a continuum. In both a philosophical and practical sense, we are what we think. We limit ourselves by what we believe is possible and our thoughts are colored by our life experiences and what we've heard.

French philosopher René Descartes, a prominent player in Western thought, said "I think; therefore I am." Witnessing ourselves think and evaluating our thoughts has much to do with the quality of life we experience and what we choose to do. The challenge to "know thyself" is not just an exercise in self-absorption; it is the key to discovering innate talents, authenticity, a sense of purpose and a passion for life. One could say that the pursuit of happiness is not external, in fact, the external rewards are often the reflection of a courageous internal journey.

From this perspective, disordered, self-destructive thinking is a calamity of major proportions. If your mind is damaged through trauma, undeveloped through neglect or chemically misfiring because of nutritional deficiencies or genetics, quality of life and even the desire to live can be severely diminished. As the physical body is directly affected by one's thoughts, imagine the physical damage resulting from unrelenting fear if one is paranoid, manic, experiencing random horrific flashbacks or obsessively worried about the unknown.

Imagine the isolation and loneliness of thinking so distorted you see people who are not there, you are split into more than one personality or live in a dissociated state. Imagine a mind so trapped in negativity and fear that despair and darkness are your only companions. We shouldn't be surprised when self-soothing of these conditions through alcohol or drugs traps people into another version of hell – addiction – or erupts into violence against self or others.

A healthy mind is our ticket to freedom, peace and joy, yet our culture has not been intentional about protecting and developing it. We are bombarded with violent and sexual images, exposed to ads telling us we aren't good enough and offered a cacophony of political voices shredding one another and filling the airwaves with fear.

As a result, our country has a high rate of incarceration, drug and alcohol use, food addiction, anxiety and depression. Researchers test sewage to determine which pharmaceuticals are in use in a community. Eighty percent of prisoners are thought to have a diagnosable mental health condition. We have a cultural, not just mental health problem.

The history of our treatment of those with mental illness, particularly those with severe symptoms, is harrowing. As neuroscience and other fields have advanced, we know so much more and have many more tools to deal with the suffering. Where once patients were chained to immovable objects, today there are medications and recovery methods that can allow them to live a more normal, albeit managed life. However, as resources have dissipated and the needs have grown, many communities have reached a crisis stage in trying to provide care.

In Fresno, emergency wards and the jail have been overwhelmed with people needing mental health treatment, leaving the afflicted to churn through these systems at great cost to the community and unimaginable personal misery. Many of the homeless are in this group of lost souls with no place to go and few to care.

Treating the symptoms of mental health conditions is the responsibility of many institutions, but none is able to or responsible for *solving* the problem. After a series of conversations convened by the Hospital Council of Northern California and a judge, applying the Four Spheres to this intractable issue made sense to a group of community leaders grappling with it.

In the early stages, the enthusiasm and commitment bode well for success. Using the Scatter Diagram, all sorts of assets and synergies have been discovered that can wrap around this challenge. Tapping into a best practice from San Antonio, Texas, we discovered a strategy that could be adapted to our unique challenges and opportunities. We already had more resources and collaborative skills than San Antonio did when it started. A community coalition, if truly committed to outcomes, is equipped not just to address the acute needs, but to head upstream and build a network to effectively manage chronic conditions, promote recovery, intervene early and advance prevention strategies. The outcomes of this effort are still pending.

While there may always be people struggling with severe diagnoses, increased understanding and more-effective tools keep changing what was once thought to be incurable into a treatable if not curable condition. Labels once considered lifelong identities are being retired as those who refused to give up found a way to heal and break free.

The Texas community leaders confirmed what many of us who have worked in the fields of addictions, justice, mental health and education already believed. The root of many mental health and addiction issues is trauma. The saying, "Genetics loaded the gun; trauma pulled the trigger," stems from this understanding.

This knowledge challenges us to focus upon prevention strategies and prioritizes early intervention. Once dysfunctional thinking and behaving become habits, mental health labels can concretize into a personality and identity, becoming far more difficult to heal.

As difficult as it is to hold people accountable for behavior resulting from inner anguish, wrapping a marshmallow of services around them rather than focusing on their ability to grow can keep them trapped. Without an authentic relationship, determining the best course of action in partnership with an individual is impossible. Recovery is a highly personal journey.

How others respond to someone experiencing a devastating event can determine whether that person grows stronger or is permanently crippled by it. Consider the child who tells someone he or she has been sexually abused. Imagine what happens if the child is immediately comforted, the perpetrator is held accountable and the child is encouraged to talk about it to anyone and as often as necessary to heal. Contrast that to the child who is hushed up and possibly punished or realizes that the adult already knew but was unwilling to help or do anything about it. How many of these children act out their pain and anger only to be judged, medicated or eventually incarcerated.

The quality of one's mental health is not simply a private matter anymore than physical health is. We all play a part in how healthy we are, how healthy those around us are and how healthy our community and culture are. Community values have a major impact in solving the challenge of mental health. Truth telling, conflict of interest, stewardship of the whole are values that have played out both as intended and as their shadow for years. Power parity is also an essential commitment.

Imagine how vulnerable someone feels who has been diagnosed with a set of labels that keep changing in the diagnostic manual based upon symptoms and influenced by a wide range of practitioners and the insurance industry. With a focus on managing the symptoms based upon drugs and certain modalities, an individual suffering from the impact of trauma may never get the help needed to heal, but rather "sentenced" to a life of chemical incarceration because it is covered by insurance. While some drugs have been a blessing, others have made a bad situation worse for suffering people while enriching a system heavily influenced by single interests.

Research shows that trauma can affect the brain's functional and chemical processing. It has demonstrated that specific nutrients and methodologies such as meditation can help it heal. Attending support groups with other trauma survivors can teach the vital skills needed to reframe experiences, process overwhelming feelings and break free from coping mechanisms that have become destructive or addictive. This is another example of how aligning the knowledge and wisdom of multiple disciplines and working together across sectors can transform thinking and actions of entire bureaucracies.

Ironically, success may also lead to a dramatic economic disruption. If those using medication and professionals choose instead the self-help, community-support route, major costs will be removed, systems of care transformed and some who have adopted labels as their identities can be restored to capable, responsible citizens. Labels, while useful as stepping stones, can too easily become prison cells offering excuses for behaviors one could change. Not everyone can, will or should take the self-help, community-support path but they offer alternatives and it is in our collective self-interest to share knowledge of them and make access widely available.

Many working in the mental health and addictions fields are drawn to them because of their own experience in trying to overcome similar challenges. Writes Robert M. Pirsig in *Lila: An Inquiry Into Morals*, a sequel to his better known classic, *Zen and the Art of Motorcycle Maintenance—An Inquiry Into Values*:

"Sometimes the insane and the contrarians and the ones closest to suicide are the most valuable people society has. They've taken the burdens of culture upon themselves, and in their struggle to solve their own problems they're solving the problems of the culture as well."

I read his first book in college, and Pirsig's father, Maynard, was my criminal law professor. Both had an interesting, if starkly different, perspective on life.

Chapter 17
PAIDEIA LOST

Paideia is a holistic approach to life-long learning with roots in ancient Greece.

There seems to be a gap in what we need from education today and the mechanisms we created yesterday to deliver it. Learning the basics, the tools of learning and communication, is still foundational, but it's become extremely important to also learn the skills of adaption, creation and resilience. As public education became more efficient and focused on measurable results, in many ways it also became less effective.

The internal side of education – know thyself, critical and creative thinking – became less important as tests focused more on facts and bubbles to fill than context, purpose and meaning. Now many leave formal education without a healthy start on basic life questions such as who am I, why am I here and what is my relationship to others? Pursuing these questions, not answers temporarily found along the way, can serve as both compass and guideposts for one's life. Most, however, were never taught how or why to pursue these questions.

Among our country's founders were philosophers, deeply reflective Renaissance thinkers who spent their lives pondering life's mysteries and trying to figure out how to build a great nation and civilization. The question, "What is our relationship to others?" follows from "Who am I?" The founders attempted to resolve these queries with a system that acknowledged the human condition and our weaknesses yet imagined a more-exalted state based upon our strengths. While their actions reflect their times in terms of their appalling treatment of Native Americans, African slaves and women, I suspect some realized they were planting seeds that they would ultimately bloom into an equality that included everyone in both thought and deed.

Ongoing debates about curriculum in public schools may well be rooted in ancient Greece, whose thinking and wisdom have heavily influenced Western civilization. Their term *paedeia* had to do with development, assisting students in achieving their highest potential reflecting their authentic nature. The Greeks believed that rhetoric, grammar, mathematics, music, philosophy, natural history and gymnastics were essential building blocks for individuals to master and govern themselves. They also focused on teaching good habits and excellence in all things, seeking to develop citizens of good character and competence. Because education was reserved for the elite, technical skills and learning a trade weren't part of the curriculum.

The divide between valuing being and doing long preceded our struggle to balance the importance of vocational and personal development. Our 21st century ideals challenge us to ensure that children's futures are not limited by circumstances of birth or the capacity of their parents. Recognizing developmental realities is essential. Many children reach adulthood lacking essential literacies. Socioeconomics often plays a role in cognitive and physical development, but material resources do not guarantee, and can sometimes compromise, ethical and spiritual development. We maintain focus on external skill sets and cognitive development without equal focus on ethics and psychological growth at our peril.

Applying Maslow's hierarchy and Jean-Paul Sartre's point that only the bourgeoisie have the luxury of navel gazing can seem like a waste of time in our high tech, fast-paced, measurement driven culture. Yet, perhaps the angst gnawing at so many who feel lost and without a purpose or connection would find solace if they realized the mere fact of sentience dooms or blesses us with the need to ask these questions.

Some turn to the answers of others and take religious teachings literally, defaulting on their responsibility to think for themselves. Others keep themselves too busy or medicated to venture inward in hopes of quelling existential torment. While thinking too much can be a problem, in today's culture the bigger problem is not thinking at all. Leaving "know thyself" out of education will not support the development of the self-actualizing and educated populace our founders believed was essential for self-governance.

If you don't know yourself, you cannot master yourself. If you have not mastered yourself, you cannot lead or manage others. The aggregate impact of our failure to do inner work is a culture searching for something on the outside we can find only within. The harm we can do to ourselves and others is all around us when we don't know who we are and respect our interdependence. Whether inspired for philosophical, spiritual and humanistic reasons or motivated by common sense and financial concerns, "right" actions and "cost effective" actions are one and the same. One need not care to connect the dots and change direction.

Gardner said it eloquently:

"In all of us there are undiscovered gifts, untested strength. Sometimes capabilities remain hidden simply because the circumstances of life do not evoke them, the challenge never arises, the call never comes. But sometimes the gifts have been buried by early defeats and harsh treatment, or layered over by cynicism, or held inactive by self-doubt. It is a matter of self-interest for every society to remove obstacles to human growth and performance. The battles we wage against physical and mental illness, prejudice, ignorance and poverty are not just exercises in compassion. They are battles for the release of human talent and energy."

Age by itself is only one factor to consider when determining a child's readiness for school. When schools include a high percentage of children whose parents lacked capacity to prepare them, this should signal an alert to school officials and community leaders that something is terribly amiss. The work to catch up and address the roots of poverty must be done simultaneously or the incoming flow will never stop. Concentrated poverty is manmade. It results from policies, once innovative, but hardened now into compliance-oriented bureaucracies and the attitudes and daily decisions of everyone who has or could have an impact upon the conditions including the economic game board.

The Fresno Business Council offers a platform to align local resources and policies to address the place-based, economic, social and educational elements of the challenge. In addition, outside resources from foundations and other levels of government will be sought to get to scale and accelerate. Aligning resources behind local strategies may well take waivers, regulatory changes and consolidations demanding leadership and political will. However, doing anything short of a full-on Blitzkrieg is doomed to fail.

Attempting to fix an academic-achievement issue in a school context is not enough in areas of concentrated poverty because attention must be paid simultaneously to all the essential factors in the Scatter Diagram to stem the tide and develop the children already in play. Stepping back in most communities, you see that most of this work is already under way in fragmented, often-competing ways. To execute a comprehensive, yet targeted approach, we need a platform wide and strong enough to focus on entire neighborhoods. The good news is most of the needed resources are available. The challenge is to inspire and sustain the attitude and behavior changes necessary to succeed in a multi-generational effort. Chronic impairments need not be permanent or inevitable if we believe, act and persevere.

With technology, rapid increases in knowledge in all disciplines and varying degrees of interest among students, determining the ideal curriculum is likely to be iterative. Unless students retain a passion for lifelong learning, they will be left behind sooner or later. Thus, students must be encouraged to think of life as the real classroom and taught that their quality of their life will be determined by choosing whether to learn or simply be entertained. As John Gardner explained:

"The ultimate goal of the educational system is to shift to the individual the burden of pursing his own education. This will not be a widely shared pursuit until we get over our odd conviction that education is what goes on in school buildings and nowhere else."

Chapter 18

LET JUSTICE RING!

When I was twelve, a college professor came to my sixth-grade class and talked about metaphysics. I was captivated and relieved. How wonderful to learn that we made everything up, that as individuals and collectively we had genesis ability. We were not victims of fate; we were the masters of our soul. We had choices, and in America we were guaranteed the freedom to make them so long as we didn't harm others and worked together to preserve it.

I decided on that day to become a philosophy major, an attorney and a writer. Already fiercely patriotic, I was determined to do my part in carrying the torch passed generation to generation to achieve the American Dream. I think of liberty and justice as bookends. When all are free from internal and external oppression, justice would be the natural outcome. Ironically, many of the most enslaved are highly educated and have material wealth. It is spiritual growth that sets us free.

Perry Mason inspired me. I wanted to be a criminal defense lawyer. It was not until I started practicing that I realized most of my clients were guilty of the charges brought and quite likely many more. To get caught, arrested and prosecuted requires a lot of people to make a decision. Reality changed my beliefs. Practicing workers compensation and personal injury law, I was struck by how crazy the system seemed. We weren't paid to help our clients in a holistic, meaningful way, but considered to be successful if they weren't held accountable or we could get them as much money as possible whether they deserved it or not. Law is linear while justice is round. Law is black and white, to be applied equally to all, while justice is often rich with ambiguity. I struggled mightily with the paradoxes and deadened my feelings until the incest case broke me open.

Before I retired from the active practice of law, we had already started exploring other ways to practice. Some attorneys would not take a drunken driving case unless the client agreed to be evaluated for alcoholism and seek help if appropriate. Getting paid to get someone off can feel like dirty money if your client kills someone the next time behind the wheel. Some attorneys require clients to enter therapy before accepting a divorce case, understanding that until people face their role in the relational breakdown, they're likely to repeat the dysfunctional behaviors or choose the same mate in a different body.

In personal injury law, finding the deepest pocket and refusing to accept responsibility for one's role in a mishap is ripe for a stewardship approach. Because much of our legal system followed the way of our politics, taxpayers ultimately pay for the lawsuit lottery against major institutions and our fear of taking action in case there may be liability. Some professionals benefit richly from the dysfunction wrought by self-interest.

Particularly damaging is our approach to individual crime. *Les Miserables* is one of our culture's favorite plays, probably because it illustrates the insanity of punishing an individual who steals a loaf of bread to feed his sister's starving child without asking why the community did nothing to remedy the situation. And of course, Victor Hugo's *Les Mis* took place in France in another century, not in the United States.

Muck-raking journalist Upton Sinclair underscored the value of Hugo's famous work by writing, "So long as there shall exist, by reason of law and custom, a social condemnation, which, in the face of civilization, artificially creates hells on earth, and complicates a destiny that is divine with human fatality; so long as the three problems of the age – the degradation of man by poverty, the ruin of women by starvation, and the dwarfing of childhood by physical and spiritual night—are not solved; so long as, in certain regions, social asphyxia shall be possible; in other words, and from a yet more extended point of view, so long as ignorance and misery remain on earth, books like this cannot be useless."

It may be satisfying to point fingers and judge, but when we do so, three fingers are pointing back at us. Individuals shouldn't escape accountability for their behavior. If, however, one is desperate or unable to respond because of brain malfunction due to trauma or lack of knowledge, how is punishment going to change the situation? It becomes a temporary and expensive fix likely to make things worse for the individual at great cost to the rest of us.

Addiction is often the result of efforts to self-soothe, and those with resources are typically able to avoid the justice system. If we're after results and a return on public investments, focusing on healing and human development makes much more sense. Sometimes ideologues and those with simple answers don't want to drill deeper because they suspect they will be implicated in some way.

The community has the right to be safe, but also has the responsibility to make sure all have opportunities. Restorative Justice is an approach based upon human development, relationship building and healing. It can yield a permanent solution as the offender is welcomed back into community after restoring relationships by making amends.

In my experience, only a tiny fraction of people are bad – dangerous sociopaths and psychopaths for whom one strike is too many. I hope to never again look into their reptilian eyes nor feel the horror of bone chill, an expression that cannot be explained, only experienced.

While those we most fear resort to violence, some of the most damaging commit white-collar crimes from their positions of power across sectors. What power they have is never enough. There are many ways to dehumanize people, all of which violate natural law, principles of justice and our country's spiritual foundations.

We built much of our justice system based upon beliefs about behavior, deciding what a crime was and what the punishment should be. Unfortunately, these decisions are rarely made impartially or holistically and now many businesses and allied interests rely on a burgeoning prison industry. If salaries of wardens and correctional officers were tied to recidivism rates, how fast would attitudes, approaches, and behaviors change and the numbers of people returning to prison dwindle? When we get better at prevention – justice on the front end – most won't end up in prison in the first place.

Smart investing in people is smart use of taxpayer's dollars. Education that prepares people for life, particularly when their family is unable to do so, is not just our collective responsibility as American citizens, it is in our self-interest.

> *"Classic economic theory, based as it is on an inadequate theory of human motivation, could be revolutionized by accepting the reality of higher human needs, including the impulse to self-actualization and the love for the highest values."* Abraham Maslow

Chapter 19

NEVER ENDING STORY

Writers have told me that the moment they finish a project, they realize they forgot something, changed their mind or have a better idea. I believe them. Attempting to do justice to the work of so many people has been a difficult task, but I'm grateful to have the story to tell.

While many are cynical, I hold to the belief that Gardner instilled in me: Americans will rise up. Apathy is not a terminal disease, only a temporary lack of faith. We can live up to our ideals and be inspired by a vision or pushed by pain and desperation. We can be asset-based and build upon our strengths or deficit-based and build bureaucracies off symptoms. We can take responsibility for the quality of our lives and our communities or dodge them, believing that someone else should step up.

This book is a call to action to those who can afford to focus on the bigger picture because far too many are simply trying to keep food on the table. I have been privileged to serve and be enriched by those who answered the call. As the only paid person in an organization that has continued to evolve for 20 years, the Fresno Business Council is testament to the fact that if a platform is available and the call is made amazing people will show up.

What we've done is provide a way for those with high-level skills honed by their work and leadership experiences to channel them into the community. We have created a place for thoughtful people to work with their peers; a platform to learn and think together, and to take actions that are intentional, aligned and impactful.

We have a long way to go before important indicators change and we are always at risk that key leaders will opt out or new ones will fail to engage. We have demonstrated the value of perseverance and we're optimistic. Younger leaders are showing up with new ideas, skills and enthusiasm. One commented at a board meeting, "Isn't stewardship just common sense?" While he got a laugh, his comment signaled the importance of renewal. Common sense stands no chance against human frailty. Without constant vigilance, our shadow side will rear its ugly head.

Eighteenth-century Irish orator John Philpot Curran is credited with originating a statement that resonates loudly for me:

> *"It is the common fate of the indolent to see their rights become a prey to the active. The condition upon which God hath given liberty to man is eternal vigilance."*

John Gardner made the point more directly:
> *"Some people need a bugle call right in the ear because this nation could die of 'comfortable indifference' to the problems citizens can solve."*

Made in the USA
San Bernardino, CA
25 November 2014